Also by James Randall Chumbley

Before the Last Dance (2006)

In the Arms of Adam: a diary of men (1997)

Alabama Snow

Alabama Snow

James Randall Chumbley

Lighted Tree Press / Atlanta

Lighted Tree Press
LightedTreePress@aol.com

Library of Congress

ISBN 978-0-9767713-1-9

Cover and author photography by Shane Booth

Select excerpts from "In the Arms of Adam: a diary of men" included.

For more information on the author:
jamesrandallchumbley.com

For Mary Ellen

No matter how far we travel from our beginnings
- whether in miles or in mind -
a part of us awaits our return.

The night before I had a dream. I was walking through the cotton fields at dusk, the buds not quite ready to bloom. The air was warm as a dwarfing fog rolled lofty and broad toward me. I was a small boy again, lost, trying to find my way back to the farmhouse; unable to see through the pallid haze, not sure which way was east or west, north or south, calling out for my mother. As I ran, unsure of my direction, the cotton thorns pricked at my skin, cutting into my flesh. The faster I ran, the deeper their sharp thorns stuck into me. My blood spilled, quickly soaked up by the ground as if the plants needed it to grow. Soon I was unable to move. Paralyzed, I stood there helpless watching the plants grow like bean stalks from a fairytale, taller and wider. Before I knew it, they had grown as high as the sky and as wide as the horizon. Within minutes I was imprisoned by millions of limbs wrapping my arms and legs, enveloping me in cotton buds. Then the plants started stretching my skin, pushing inward until they punctured my flesh, growing into me until I was one with the cotton.

Alabama Snow

Love is a fragile thing between husband and wife, child and parent, between siblings, and between lovers. It can make you strong and bring joy into your life, or it can destroy your heart and soul.

Introduction

Rarely does it snow in the South. Like most things in life, all the right elements have to come into play for it to happen; those right elements are not common in this region of the country. Although, when it does, it is incredibly magical, especially to a little boy isolated in a world of pain, confusion and chaos. Suddenly, that world turns into a fairytale winter wonderland. For a moment anything seems possible. There is a sense of hope despite the surrounding darkness and despair of days that never see light. Nothing matters except for the snow. The turmoil of life is forgotten for a brief period while the snow falls—as if a gift from the heavens—with billions of individual white, airy flakes, carrying hope and promise down to the cold earth. That black world turns white: the ground, the trees, the bushes, the houses, the cars, and the streets. White on white on white. Everything seems pure and good, regardless of what is underneath its blanket—and most of all—calm and quiet. The snow has a way of silencing the strife inside, as the neighborhood gradually fills with the joyous, muffled voices of children playing in an unexpected wonderland as that little boy watches from the picture window of the house that chaos built.

As a child, the first snow I knew about, other than from magazine pictures and movies and the month of December picture of the large wall calendar that hung in the kitchen next to the stove, was that which grew out of the ground and was anything but cold. It comes in the fall, not the winter months. It looked like snow, but it was cotton. Even when I saw my first real snowfall, I was taken back to the first time I saw what I thought was snow in the wandering fields of my grandfather's farm in Alabama from the window of the car, my father at the wheel, as it raced over the road taking us back to where it all began for her—my mother.

"Look, Mommy, it's snow!" I screamed in excitement as I looked out from the car.

"It's a different kind of snow, Dear," she told me.

"Can we go out and play in it?"

"No. It's not that kind of snow."

Since that memory, and that childhood, the years have moved faster than that speeding car, and I have traveled on countless roads. I have seen many snowfalls—from the wet, wintry ones of Germany where I lay down to make winged angels beside my mother, the icy cold, infrequent ones in Middle Georgia, and the ones which cover the tops of the majestic mountains of Big Bear, California. At the first sight of any snowfall, no matter where I may be, I am always taken back to those fields covered in white and back to memories of my mother when she was young and full of hopes and dreams. Now that she is no longer physically here, I have to call on those memories stored in my mind and on photographs. One in particular: a beautiful, young girl standing in a field of cotton—Alabama Snow.

Many of the pictures of her youth haunt me; a swell of them pushing out of an open box, in no particular order, of various sizes and clarity. They were taken long before she carried me in her womb, and in a time so different than the one in which I was born. The world was in turmoil outside the little town that seeded her and her dreams. She looks different in the pictures than how I remember her after she brought me into this world; when I was just a little boy, following her around holding on to her full-flowing skirts—like holding on to a lifeline. She was unambiguously my world as most mothers are to their young children. I would not have life if not for the sacrifices she made. She gave up a part of herself—a most precious part—surrendering a piece of her soul so another could exist. And because of her relinquishing, something left her, a vital part, and, after it was gone, she changed.

I like her better in the pictures that seem to convey promise and a bright future. Her eyes are clear and wide in many of the images as if ready to take in every visual aspect of life. Her smile appears hopeful that the past will stay behind and not follow as she moves forward and away from the stormy events that plagued the innocence of the little girl she once was. As I study the photographs, it seems as if those eyes are drawing me in, and now that her physical presence has departed, they want to tell me the story of how and why she ended up the way she did. She wants me to know and, more importantly, understand.

I want to know, too. She deserves for that story to be uncovered.

In order to do so, I have to pull together the bits and pieces of her life; like gathering the scattered parts of a puzzle, which will hopefully show a more complete picture of the woman who gave me life. As most sons believe they know their mothers, for the longest time I thought I knew her as well. But, as I sit on the floor surrounded by boxes that are now the guardians of the archives of her journey, I find that I did not know her as well as I had once thought.

I will go back to where it all began for her, and walk over the footsteps of her youth that have long been smoothed away with the passing of time. I will stand in a yard where she once played and looked up at the trees that gave her shade. And, if some of those trees are gone, then I will stand under the ones that came from their seeds. I will walk along the road that leads to the place she called home, and that led her away. It may have been covered in dirt and gravel, but it is one she paved with her own hopes and dreams for a life far away. I will breathe the air, and smell the faint aromas that linger from her childhood: the dirt from the farm, the oak, the wild flowers, and the tall grasses that blow in the wind. And, most of all, I will stand where she once did and listen to the narrow, soft-flowing creek as it meanders not far from the road, but hidden by an assortment of oddly shaped trees—both tall and wide—down a gently sloping hill. It is there that I will meet her again.

I have often imagined what her early years were like. It seems easier for me to think about those years than dwell on the troubled ones I lived with her. It is too difficult—beyond painful—to remember the sadness, fear and loneliness that were too often evident on her face. So, I choose to go back and search out the girl that became the woman. A woman, despite the odds which she faced, who held on to hope until the very end.

I know some of the story of her childhood, but it is incomplete. My mother never really talked much about what it was like growing up in poverty. My uncle once told me: *We were poor, but Mary Ellen never acted poor.* Besides her physical beauty, she had the intellectual potential to break away from the farm life she detested. Now, I will search out the truth, and rekindle the dreams and hopes that danced in a little girl's eyes as she overcame great odds to find moments of happiness.

Prologue

She sits at a quaint bistro table on the narrow sidewalk. The aged unleveled concrete is wet from the hosing by a muddled-haired restaurant employee, wearing a crisp red apron embellished with the establishment's logo—103 Cafe—in a cream color, dead in its center. It is a luminous, late morning, close to lunchtime. Her back is to the eleven o'clock sun to keep it out of her sensitive eyes. The back of her pale neck and arms, exposed by the short-sleeves of her green flower-print dress, are warmed by it. The air smells clean as she takes a deep breath without being aware of its intensity. Her lungs expand and then discharge the spent air. She considers pulling a cigarette from the generic, half-emptied pack positioned on the table close to her glass of white wine, but keeps her hands in her lap. She is distracted for a moment from the calming thought of a cigarette by an odd-looking man leisurely riding past on a junky bicycle. He smiles at her and signals with the bell on the handlebars. To her, he looks like a circus performer, but he is not. He is just an odd-looking man in mismatched clothes. Somehow she feels like she knows him, not in a social way, but more from life experience. There is a kinship that is evident to her, and she thinks to him, too, as she returns the smile, but it is one in passing, and he has acknowledged that bond with the ring. The front wheel wobbles as the cyclist returns to his concentration, maneuvering his transportation forward. She is amused and watches him until he is out of sight.

There is activity encompassing her: people walking up and down the sidewalk on both sides of the narrow street, their muffled conversations about life or just the day ahead croon in the air around the white-haired woman, as a few cars slowly drive by with their occupants looking onward. The smell of baking bread with the suggestion of cinnamon, mixed with other flavors from the café, encircle her as she seizes another profound inhale, enjoying the delicious aromas.

Her short hair, thinned by the years, is white like the first fallen snow of winter, and almost straight, except for a slight curl that frames her sweet, aging face. Her eyes are still young, although they have seen much sadness. Her heart, the same, as it has felt the same melancholy. But today there is a lean smile on the thinning lips of that face. Perhaps incited by her passing admirer on the bike or, more likely, she feels a succinct sense of freedom. She is a stranger here; just arriving within the past few hours on a dust-covered, road-wearied Greyhound bus that brought her through the night.

It would be a rare coincidence—more close to impossible—that anyone around would know her or of the weighty past she carries with her that has slowed her journey through life, and of the past she protects as a lioness would protect its young. Now, she is living in the present for whatever time she will sit at the little bistro table on the slim sidewalk watching the wet pavement dry. Although close to an impracticable task, she will try not to think about the past or the future. Instead, the white-haired lady will, for the first time in many years of her adult life, live in the moment.

She removes the silver Timex watch from her wrist and places it in the modest black handbag sitting in the empty chair at the table next to the single, mid-sized piece of blue canvas luggage. It is a subconscious movement—removing the watch—to slow, perhaps stop time, so she can sit and enjoy the warmth of the late morning sun on her. The white-haired woman reaches for the glass of wine marked by a faint impression of her lips in red. It is a splendid day she thinks, as she sits as an observer, watching the world go by. Yes, she will live in the moment and not think about yesterday—or even tomorrow until it comes.

The Dress

I walk to the full-length glass front door, standing there looking out toward the street. Just standing, waiting in my bare feet, shirtless, in my white briefs, hoping his silver Corolla would pull up in front of the house. Then he would run up the walk and I would meet him on the porch. He would wrap his arms around me and kiss me on the lips, hard and long. He would look into my eyes and say he was sorry. He would tell me he loves me. Night after night I stood there in the shadows of a dark house waiting for that moment. Surely he would come back. The last two years were not a dream. They were real. He would realize that and he would be back. Yes, they were real, alive, we experienced them together. We lived them! Every moment. Again, surely he was coming back.

Then the mourning began, and with it the unbearable

pain took over what was left of my life. My life had caught up with me—fifty plus years were choking me around the neck...

The day before the funeral, I had a horrific fight with my sister over what to dress our mother in for her new journey. I wanted something familiar from her closet, something she had loved to wear, something I had bought for a birthday, or Mother's Day, or perhaps Christmas. I wanted the dress to mean something, to represent a moment of an event in my mother's life that made her smile—to mean something other than death. But Sandra wanted something new.

In truth, the disagreement over the dress was an excuse to "open the flood gates." The fight was not about the dress, but about madness, disappointments, shame, and fear. It was about who loved our mother more and whom our mother loved the best. It was about a lifetime of pain and heartache—our mother's. And it was about the guilt—our guilt that was eating at our very cores, eating us from the inside out that we could not save her; we had been too busy trying to save ourselves from the past—our childhoods. The more we fed the guilt, the weaker we became and unable to keep our personal rage contained. It resulted in a harsh, name-calling fight in the front yard of our mother's modest house on that bleak, foggy November morning.

I thought we had exchanged every possible hateful word earlier inside the house, and even on the days prior, but Sandra followed me outside with more to say. Our uncle, my mother's younger brother, stood stoically, with an indignant look on his face. Siggy, her friend—a petite, confident, athletic, energy-filled woman of German descent with strong religious convictions—watched speech-less in the doorway with him. I stood on the short, brown grass that covered the front yard. The air felt cold and soggy in the early hour, as I glared at my sister standing in the center of the front porch, still in her night-clothes and her housecoat hanging open, with a half-smoked cigarette in her fingers. Every few seconds, between outbursts of rage, she would take a nervous, sporadic drag off the ciga-rette, and then comb her messy, brown, slightly graying hair with her other hand.

"You controlling bitch! I've had all I can take of you!" I screamed, as I turned toward my Rover.

"You're the fucking bitch!" my sister refuted. "I'm the one who took care of Mother these last few years while you and Steven could not have cared less about us."

"No. You're impossible. And I took care of her while you were away in the Army for twenty years! You seemed to have forgotten about that, Sister. I gave up my dream of moving to California! Who would have taken care of her then, if I had gone?"

My sister had retired several years ago, deciding to move back to Warner Robins and in with our mother, partly out of guilt of being away for so long, but I know she wanted to help our mother, too. It was the helpless helping the helpless, and too big of a task for one person alone. Although they loved each other, or whatever they thought love was, many times they were at each other's throats unable to let the past die, of which we had all been guilty. Mother really should have been in an assisted liv-ing situation after having been released from the State Mental Hospital in Milledgeville several years before San-dra's retirement. Although it had been highly recom-mended, Mother refused to leave her house.

"I came home for visits, and Mother came to see me at times," Sandra justified.

"It's not the same. You were gone. Steven was unavailable. He only took over legal guardianship to try to keep Mother under wraps when she went into the State Hospital."

"Whatever! I hate you, Randy. I hate you!"

"Yeah, at least I didn't try to kill Mother by spiking her booze with blood pressure medication! You could have killed her! Oh, wait. That's what you were trying to do. Kill her!" I yelled out of anger, knowing that Sandra really did not intentionally try to kill our mother; they had both been drinking a lot during Mother's illness and her medications were not supposed to be taken with alcohol. But our mother was very demanding at times, and could be unrelenting when it came to getting her liquor when she wanted it regardless of the warnings from the doctors.

At that point we were both crying, as the anger spewed in the form of ugly words from our mouths like thick repulsive vomit, some of what was barely audible as it was slurred between gasps of breaths.

I threw the bag I had over my shoulder into the back of the Rover and slammed the tailgate. All I could think about was getting out of this wretched place and back to Atlanta. In my haste, and present contempt for my sister, I had convinced myself I did not need to be at my mother's funeral, that she would understand my absence. With everything that had happened, I just could not stomach what was left of my family anymore, now that the best part was gone. I jumped into the driver's seat, crammed the key into the ignition, and, in reverse, sped out of the driveway with the door partly open. I slowed down at the end of the block just enough to pull it shut before turning the corner.

I passed the old high school and drove until I got to the railroad tracks where I was forced to stop by the red light at the main road leading to the highway. I was trembling in my seat. Atlanta was only ninety-eight miles north, but it seemed like a million. I had had enough and wondered if the misery would ever end, and if I would ever be freed from the family dynamics that magnified my human flaws and short comings.

"Come on, damn it, change," I cursed the light out loud, thinking to myself, if it did not in another second I will run it.

"Finally!"

I slammed my foot on the gas pedal. The Rover noisily rocked and rattled over the double tracks, speeding onto the highway, exceeding the limit by twenty miles an hour.

"I'm done with this place," I spoke out loud again, talking to myself like a crazy person. "I'm done. The hell with my sister and brother, too!"

Then the guilt started eating at me again.

"I'm going to miss my mother's funeral."

"It's okay, she will understand."

It was like I split into two different people. One telling me it was okay; to keep going. The other, to turn the Rover around.

"But you have to go back. You're giving the eulogy. You have to!"

"They won't listen to it anyway. Keep going to Atlanta. You don't belong back there anymore. You haven't in a long, long time. Keep going!"

"But, then who will stand up for her? They have to know the truth!"

"They don't care about the truth!"

"You care. Don't you care that they know? You have to

go back! They have to hear the truth and face it one last time."

My cell phone rang on the passenger seat.

"Don't answer it. It's probably your sister. You're done with her. You're done!"

I looked at the phone until it stopped ringing. Then turned my eyes back to the highway.

"Keep going."

The phone rang again.

"Pick it up. See who it is!"

I reached for the phone. The name Siggy was flashing in the little window.

"Hello."

"Are you okay?" she asked, in a tender voice.

"No, I'm not. I'm sorry you had to witness the fight."

"Are you really going back to Atlanta and miss your mother's funeral?"

"I don't know what I'm doing, Siggy."

There was a pause.

"I'm going to the mall to get your mother a dress. I'll take care of it. Okay?"

We were both silent for a minute.

"No. No," I thought for a few seconds more.

"You have to turn back," said the other voice in my head.

"I'll meet you there, Siggy."

I had always picked out clothes for my mother. She said I had good taste. I could not let her down now.

"Okay, drive carefully, Randy. Meet me at Belk's."

Illegally, I crossed over the median at a level spot, a good reason to drive a Range Rover, and headed back.

Ten minutes later, I pulled into the parking lot as Siggy was getting out of her car. I had stormed out of the house, in such a rush to get away, without a shower or even a quick attempt to groom myself. I grabbed a Falcon's baseball cap off the back seat to cover my bed-head. Clearly I was not dressed for the weather in flip-flops and a T-shirt. The chilly air hit me as I opened the Rover's door. Earlier, in the yard, I was too overheated emotionally to notice the cold. I stuck my hands deep into my jeans' pockets, to warm them, as I hurried to where Siggy was standing.

We did not speak of the fight as we walked through the glass front doors into the store bejeweled in a celebration of Christmas, but it was on both our minds. Siggy looked obviously cautious and concerned, and I could see the alarm on her face. My fight with Sandra had troubled her. I was still shaken and ashamed of the show my sister and I had performed for an unwilling audience. A grouping of tall, snow-flocked trees with oversized red, shiny balls greeted us as holiday music filled the store, enticing customers into the mood to buy gifts for loved-ones, while employees with Santa hats scampered around—like jumbo elves—industriously preparing for the after-Thanksgiving Day sale to come. We wandered into the ladies department and through the racks of clothes. I felt sick to my stomach as I tried to pretend I was shopping for gifts for my mother for Christmas; shopping for things I hoped would put a smile on her face, even though I was looking for a dress in which to bury her.

Nothing in the sea of racks of hanging garments seemed suitable. I knew this would be the last gift I would ever purchase for my mother. The last dress. I remembered back to those past birthdays, Mother's Days and Christmases—to that look on her face when she held a present in her lap. The smile of anticipation on her lips was warming to my heart. She would look at the gift as long as possible before I prodded her to open it. In those few moments she stared at the gift, I am sure her mind went through a list of possibilities of what was hidden in the wrapped box on her lap. Those moments were precious—those moments of possibilities.

I knew there was a dress here somewhere. The one dress, the final dress she would have loved to wear. I had to find it. I had to find it for her.

Black Cats & Monsters

It was impossible to sleep the night before the funeral. I was still upset over the fight with my sister and had done my best to avoid her after returning from the mall. The house had always been small, but that night it seemed even smaller. It felt like the walls were closing in on me and I was in a doll house. Everything was uncomfortable: the room, the bed, the temperature, the darkness; even the silence of a house that for years I had hated and, more so, the events that it concealed; in a place erroneously referred to as home. It never felt like home or what I thought a home should feel like. But how would I know? How would I know what a home was supposed to feel like? It was the place I came back to year after year like a migratory animal. The route was ingrained—instinctive. I came out of obligation and love, but mostly obligation. I came

31

because I was from her and I knew as long as my mother was there, I would have to continue to return. After the service, there would not be a reason for another homecoming ever again. In an odd way I felt some sense of relief, some kind of new sovereignty. Finally, I might be free to never have to return to the city, to the house, or to the room I detested. My regret—my mother was never able to leave except by death.

Then the realization hit me like a truck barreling down the highway of life. Suddenly I felt weak, small, powerless. The realization: at fifty-one years old, I reverted back to a boy, and I had done so each and every time I walked into this house after the day I had moved out. I turned on the lamp beside the bed and fought with its adjustable arm that refused to bend in the right direction to keep the light from shining in my eyes. After a fruitless struggle I gave up and left it on; too afraid to lie awake in a black room. Yes, I was a grown man too afraid to lie awake in the dark where monsters were able to run amuck. I have never been a fan of the night and still sleep with a light on when I am alone; always a soft light, which comforts me by keeping the suffocating darkness at bay.

Even as a little boy I felt I was surrounded by these monsters. In my mind they were always within inches of me at every moment—in the closet, under the bed, behind the door—but were powerless in the daylight. I could always run, or at least see where I was running. Once darkness took over, the monsters had free range and could easily surround me, leaving me without a route of escape. And the biggest, meanest and scariest monster of them all was my father.

I turned my back to the lamp and stared at the vacant, white wall. For most of the night, I found every minor imperfection: every crack, every mark, every dent and blemish that most people would never notice in passing. But I was not "passing by." I had returned one final time; perhaps I was trapped, or I had come full circle. Regardless, thirty-plus years had come and gone since I had slept in that room on a regular basis. Thirty-plus years and now I was back as if nothing had changed, and my biggest concern at the moment—I feared I had not changed as well. It was like I had never packed a bag and carried it out the front door. Nothing had happened since the day I thought I had walked away. I had such high hopes of getting away—far away and never returning. Rather, I had never walked away, but had been asleep all those years in the same bed, in the same room, in the same house. Now, I was wide-awake.

One of my mother's three cats scratched at the door. Persistently it scratched for some attention; perhaps looking for her—looking for my mother. Briefly it gave up and, I am sure, went to my mother's room across the hall where my uncle and aunt were sleeping with the door closed. Unable to disturb them, the cat returned. It scratched and cried softly, patiently, sympathetically, until I got out of bed and opened the door just enough so it could pop its head through. It was Denny, the black one, her favorite. The cat looked up at me, seemingly disappointed I was not my mother. Then Denny squeezed the rest of her body through and ran under the bed.

It was odd—the cat coming into the room with me. I fully expected her to continue her search elsewhere. Denny liked only my mother. She usually kept a comfortable distance, hissing at anyone that came near, including the other two cats and the dog that Mother adopted after her, as well as Sandra's dog, Dallas. I returned to the bed and faced the wall again. My mind was wandering and the random thoughts seemed to be ricocheting off the inside of my skull. I suddenly remembered the surprise afternoon phone call from my mother years earlier. Her voice was clear in my head.

"Guess what I did today, Son?" my mother asked.

"Tell me, Mother, what did you do?"

"No, guess. You have to guess."

"Okay. You dyed your hair green?" I humored her.

"No, silly," she laughed.

"Purple, then?"

"You'll never guess," she taunted.

"Well, then tell me," I insisted.

"I went to the Humane Society and got a cat."

"What did you say?"

I almost fell off my chair, close to choking on the partially-chewed bite of turkey sandwich I was eating. Mother never liked cats. I can even remember her saying she out-right, unequivocally detested them.

"Yes!"

"You're right. Never in a million, no, make that a billion years would I have guessed that, Mother. But, you're kidding, right?" I coughed, trying to clear my airway.

"No. I'm not kidding. I got a cat. Her name is Denny. She's a black cat," she said proudly.

"Aren't black cats bad luck?" And they were, almost, for me at that moment.

"Only if they cross your path," Mother smirked.

"Whatever moved you to get a cat? I thought you hated them," I questioned after a swallow of soda.

"I was watching the *Today Show* this morning and there was a guest talking about adopting animals. The man said people who have pets live longer."

"I've heard that, too, but you'll outlive all of us, Mother."

She went on to inform me that very morning, after the show, she called one of her friends to take her to the animal shelter, then to Kmart to get food, litter and a box. It was the beginning of the love affair between Denny and Mother. And I mean—a love affair!

In some way, I understood why. She wanted more time. More time to start living the life she had put on hold for her husband and children. I could see her reasoning: if a so-called expert said a pet would help her live longer, then she would get one, especially if it meant more time to live her dreams, if only in her imagination. Denny was her medicine and quickly became her world. Mother believed that the cat somehow knew she had saved her from being destroyed. It was a win-win for both of them, for Mother and Denny. Over time, two more cats showed up in her life. JoAnn, the lady that delivered Mother's Meals On Wheels, told her about a cat named Emmy in need of a good home. Then, the lost kitten that was lucky enough to wander onto Mother's front porch, she named Donnie. In-between Emmy and Donnie, there came Suzie, the run away Yorkie.

They became Mother's entourage; her family. A source of unconditional love she had never felt or experienced from any other creature, including from her children, until her pets. Quickly she grew in constant fear of losing them, but she really was afraid of losing love. Denny and Suzie had gotten out several times after she first got them. Quickly, a new house rule was established by Mother: before anyone could come in or out of the house, the pets had to be rounded up in the back bedroom or laundry room. I once had to chase Suzie ten blocks before I caught her. That Yorkie was notorious for running. One would think that dog had Greyhound blood in its veins because every chance it got—it was gone. Mother often said she would die if anything ever happened to them because they loved her more than her children could, and they did not judge her as others had.

Denny meowed under the bed. My throat became scratchy and my nose stuffy. I got up and made my way to the kitchen, softly lit by the flickering florescent light over the sink. Denny stayed behind. I rummaged through the cabinet where mother kept all her medicines—shelf after shelf from front to back of crowded prescriptions for depression, anxiety, sleeping, blood pressure, heart medications, constipation, antibiotics, and on and on. I grabbed a glass from the plastic dish rack next to the sink, filling it with water from the faucet, before popping a Benadryl and a sleeping pill, hoping I would fall asleep. When I returned to the bedroom, Denny leered at me from under the bed. She stayed there the rest of a wakeful night until the light in the room grew brighter, telling me the day was approaching.

I rolled over to turn out the table lamp. It was cold, but the coolness was coming from inside of me and I felt groggy from the leftover affects of the Benadryl and sleeping pill. I sat up in bed. I could hear my uncle and aunt talking as they walked back and forth between my mother's bedroom and the bathroom getting dressed, and I smelled the pot of coffee they had started. Their voices were unsteady and hushed as they had a discussion about driving back to Fayette, Alabama after the service. I did not want them to leave; it was like a part of my mother was leaving again, too.

I stood up and waited for the morning dizziness to subside before moving in slow motion toward my bag of clothes and the suit hanging on the closet door. I had taken a shower the night before, so all I needed to do was wash my face, brush my teeth and comb some water through my hair before dressing. I grabbed a few things from the bag and waited for my uncle and aunt to finish in the bathroom. Once partially clothed, I looked around the house. In a few weeks everything would be gone; it would be an empty house. I wondered where the monsters would go. Sandra had arranged for an estate seller to tag all the furniture and belongings that we were not keeping to be sold. There was a pending sale on the house as well; one of the neighbors down the street had agreed to buy it. I went back to my room and sat down on the edge of the bed holding the loose sheets of paper on which I had written my mother's eulogy. I felt ice cold again. Thirty-plus years ago I sat on the bed in that very room the night before I moved out, worried about leaving Mother alone. That day had come, again. This time, it was the day before Thanksgiving.

Déjà vu

Images of my mother flashed on the large flat screen television in the funeral home greeting room spanning the seventy-five years of her life. A few days before the fight, Sandra and I had spent hours going through boxes of pictures until we had collected fifty—fifty pictures that captured countable moments of our mother's lifetime. One-after-the-other, the images appeared on the screen as serene music played in the background. At a snail's pace, I walked toward the bronze casket carrying a large, previously-used gift bag filled with stuff—mementos of that life to put in the casket with her body. My college diploma—that I had given to my mother the day I graduated. I went for her, not for myself. It was important to her; I would have preferred to go to California after high

39

school instead. Two Anne Murray CDs. Several copied photographs of my brother, sister and me from child-hood—one of us standing on a playground—and of Mother in her youth and as a young woman full of life. Hand-fulls of Mother's Day and birthday cards I had given her over the years which she had saved. Letters I wrote trying to encourage her to believe in herself again. A silly stuffed black cat toy, resembling Denny, that I had given her the last time she went in the hospital. One by one, I placed the items in her casket as I tried to take hold of my emotions and the anger spilling out of my being. I talked to my mother, fully aware that she was not in that body anymore. The make-up artist had done a good job, but the woman in the casket did not look like the woman I had called Mother. However, she had been sick for a long time and not herself. Somehow, the unlikeness was com-forting.

I placed a bouquet of yellow roses in her hands folded on her stomach. The day before I went back to Atlanta to get my friend Theodora to help me make one for Mother as well as one for each of her closest friends to be given out as they arrived at the service. The roses look vibrant against the emerald-green (her favorite color) high-necked dress. The long-sleeves of the accompanying black, short-waisted jacket covered the bruises on her arms from all the intravenous needles. As soon as I saw the dress at Belk's, I knew my mother's eyes would have lit up once she unwrapped it.

"Merry Christmas, Mother," I softly spoke, as I leaned over to kiss her cheek.

I began sobbing. Grief rolled down my cheeks. I scooped-up the tears from my face with my fingers and wiped them on her lips.

Sandra had stayed outside to smoke a cigarette. Uncle Ben and Aunt Jerry sat side-by-side on a plush sofa positioned against the wall in the entrance. After a few quiet moments of regaining some composure, I took a seat in the greeting room to watch the images of my mother flash on the big screen. It was almost as big as those at a movie theater. "You should have been in the movies," I whispered, as if Mother was sitting next to me on the sofa. "You could have been a star."

From the corner of my eye I saw two figures approaching. I turned my head slightly to see my older brother, Steven; his large, rounded frame stopped in front of me. I crooked my neck up. He stood there seemingly undecided as to whether to sit or keep moving. It was an uncomfortable moment for both of us. His tie was loose around the collar of his light-blue, small-boxed patterned shirt. The navy jacket he was wearing was opened wide, being held back by his hands in the pockets of his khaki slacks. Carl, his son, tagged behind, his head timidly down. He was as tall as his father, six-one or so, pudgy and handsome. As with all of my brother's children, I had seen him only three or four times over the years. Carl was nineteen now. Awkwardly they took a seat on the sofa across from me. I was shocked to see Carl, and that meant his two sisters and Steven's wife, Rachel, would most likely be coming to the service as well. The thought was distressing. I could feel my face turning red with anger. I felt the heat begin to rise up in me, first from my chest, to my neck and finally until my face was flush. I became redder and redder, not needing a mirror to see. Within minutes, my flesh was burning.

A year ago, I had strongly suggested to Steven that he have his children visit their grandmother in the hospital or call or send her a card now and then. At the very least, pretend they cared. The oldest, Debra, and the middle-child, Alice, just as their brother, were old enough to understand why Mother was the way she was. My suggestion was ignored. Not once in the two years Mother was ill did the grandchildren make an attempt to contact her.

All I could do was sit there and look past them. I knew it was pointless to say anything at that moment. If I did, it would only end in another argument at the expense of our mother. I tried my best to be civil to my brother and his son, but it was hard to contain the anger on my face and in the pit of my stomach.

"Wow, Carl. You're all grown. How are you?"

"I'm good," he uttered, looking down at his fingers fidgeting in his lap.

What else could he say? I was basically a stranger. As far as my brother was concerned, we had nothing in common except our mother; and I was still trying to get past the worst insult he had done to her.

The day after our mother went into the coma, I drove back to Atlanta for a night to take care of some of my personal affairs. The next day on my drive back to Warner Robins, Steven called, informing that our sister had been sent home from the hospital for being intoxicated. I was disappointed, but far from surprised. One of mother's faithful friends took Sandra home. Steven had been calling our sister, but she was not picking up the phone and he was concerned she might go back to get her car. I had planned on going directly to the hospital, but told him I would go by the house first to check on our sister.

The brakes of the Rover squeaked as it came to a halt in the driveway covered in a heavy blanket of multiple-colored leaves fallen from the surrounding trees. They stirred under my footsteps as I made my way across the sleepy lawn. The air was tepid as I walked up the brick steps to the porch of the house. Plants in several pots were slumped over from the blast of colder weather a few nights ago and from a lack of watering. Regrettably, I knew what I would most likely find on the other side of the door. I felt like I was walking back in time. I put my key in the lock and took a deep breath. The door was out-of-plumb and stuck at the bottom. I turned the knob hard up and pushed inward. Immediately, a screen of smoke greeted me. My sister's hazy image was sitting across the room on the sofa. Sandra was drunk. A can of beer in her hand, as she sat in the living room on the dog-worn sofa—in the very spot where our father had shot himself over three decades ago. I could smell the beer on her breath from where I was standing a good six feet away. It was potent, enough to tell me she had been drinking all day, and, by the look of things, she was not ready to stop for the night. The light in the room was dim, despite the intense lit bulb of the lamp on the table against the wall, causing Sandra's body to cast a monstrous shadow on the brick divider that separated the living and dining rooms. The cigarette smoke became chunkier in the air as I approached her. The room smelled damp and dusty as I was forced to breathe it into my lungs. What was left of a six-pack of canned-beer was on the floor at her feet. All I could think about was Mother in the coma and Sandra was just adding so much more stress and misery to an already dire situation.

"Why are you doing this?" I asked, as I stopped a few feet in the front of her.

"I'm an alcoholic," her words slurred, as she lifted the beer to her lips.

She took a big slurp and held the can to her lips, ready to take a second. Sandra's eyes were unfocused and watery, her hair a rat's nest and her clothes mismatched and wrinkled. Her mascara had bled under her eyes making her look like a raccoon, her lipstick was smeared, and the heavily applied blush made her look like a circus clown.

"I know you're an alcoholic, but our mother is in the hospital," I raised my voice in disappointment and disgust.

"Leave me alone!"

"I can't. Think about Mother. You promised her you would stay sober."

"Leave me alone!" she repeated.

"You're heading down the same road as Mother. Look where it led her."

Guardedly, I took the last few steps to where she was sitting. I looked down at her unsure of my feelings, unsure if I pitied her, or was disgusted by her drunken condition. Instinctively, I reached for the remaining beer on the floor. Sandra staggered up from the sofa and grabbed the plastic rings that held the cans together. We began a tug-of-war for the beer, both yelling—me to let go and her to let her drink and leave her alone. I wanted to leave her alone. I had had enough of the drinking—my father's, my mother's and Sandra's. Enough! We both were unrelenting in our objective. She was just as determined to keep the beer as I was to take it from her. It was déjà vu. I had done this for years with our mother—pouring out the beer and watering down the wine and hard stuff. I felt helpless again. I was unable to save my mother, and I knew I could not save my sister. But that did not stop me from holding on to the beer. Instead I became more enraged. Hopping mad, not just at the situation of my sister drunk on the sofa in the very spot where our father had killed himself, but because of why he killed himself. Mostly because of his madness fueled by alcohol, and what it and the alcohol had done that played a role in putting our mother in the hospital and aided in ending her life. My anger took over. It erupted as Sandra reached for my arm, digging her fingernails into my flesh. I slapped her across the face. She stood there frozen. Stunned, she sat back down. I had slapped her hard. It was truly déjà vu. Years earlier, I had slapped my mother because of her drinking and the same irate behavior it produced; the madness that ran in our mother's veins was raging in my sister's and mine. At that moment, I was fighting with all of them—my father, mother and sister.

Defeated in more ways than one, Sandra put her hand to the red spot on her face. Meekly she surrendered the beer. I took it to the kitchen and emptied the remaining cans in the sink before checking the refrigerator and cabinets to see if there was any more. I returned to the living room to find her mumbling something to herself and looking off in the distance.

"I think you should go to bed," I said in as much of a sympathetic tone as I could muster. I wanted not to care, and a small part of me did not, but I was not made of stone as much as I may have wanted to be at that moment.

"I hate you," Sandra said, as she turned her head, glaring up at me with the same look in her eyes that I had seen in our mother's time and time again.

"I hate you," she repeated.

I had heard the same words before, too, from her and our mother. And if eyes could kill, then I should have dropped dead at that very instant, cold-stone-dead. They always hated me for pouring out the alcohol. Although, I never poured out my father's, I was not that brave. He

45

would have killed me for sure.

Sandra stood up, staggering into me. I reached out my hand to steady her.

"Don't touch me!" she warned.

I followed Sandra into her bedroom as she took calculated steps to keep her balance. Her Springer Spaniel, Dallas, was already in the bed. Sandra began baby-talking to him as she sulked slowly next to him.

"At least you love me, don't you, Dallas?" she said, as a jab directed at me.

"I love you, too. Why else would I bother?" I corrected her, really not sure if I did or not. But I felt sorry for her. Maybe feeling sorry was what love was in our family.

"I'm going to the hospital to spend the night. You get some sleep and call me on my cell in the morning."

"No, I'm going with you," Sandra said, as she tried to get out of bed.

"No! No! You stay and sleep it off. You spent the night last night. You need to sleep."

Sandra lay back next to Dallas. He licked her face.

"Do you know why I got drunk today?" she asked.

"I know why you got drunk. You can't control yourself. Not even at a time like this when I need you to be strong. We have to be strong for each other. It's what Mother would have wanted us to do."

"No. I got drunk because of the baby."

"Because of the baby? What baby?" I questioned, thinking she was talking nonsense.

"Yes," she slurred. "This morning one of the nurses at the hospital asked me how the baby was doing," my sister explained.

"How the baby was doing? What are you talking about?" I asked, puzzled.

46

"I asked the nurse what baby?" Sandra said.

"Steven's grandbaby," the nurse clarified.

"Steven's a grandfather? When did that happen?"

"The nurse told me that Debra had a baby earlier in the year sometime. I called Steven from the waiting room and he told me it was true. He never told Mother or me."

"Unbelievable!" I said shaking my head.

"I asked Steven why he never told us. He said he thought I would be upset because of the abortion I had many years ago," Sandra explained, still slurring her words.

"So, our poor mother, in a coma, doesn't know she's a great-grandmother?"

"No. Can you believe it?"

"It's bull shit. And, yes ... now that I know about it, I can. And it's still bull shit."

"Yeah. At least we agree on that."

"I'm sorry, but it's no reason to get drunk, especially with Mother in a coma."

"Whatever."

"What is it? Boy or girl, I mean."

"A girl."

"What's her name? Wait, don't tell me. I don't want to know right now."

Sandra closed her eyes. I stood there for a few minutes trying to digest what I had just learned. The anger I felt for my sister shifted toward Steven. How could he keep that from his own mother? In my mind, it was unforgivable. Our mother had been in-and-out of the hospital for two years and he had kept something—a huge gift—that would have brought her some happiness; the knowledge of a great-grandchild.

"I really need to head to the hospital," I said, as I turned to walk out of the room.

"Randy."

"What?"

"Nothing."

"I love you," I said again because I thought she wanted to hear the words, and because of our mother; even if I did not know what the words really meant anymore.

Sibling Rivalry

I hurried out to the Rover. I felt the blood racing through my veins like I had been hit by lightning. I could understand Steven not telling me about Debra's baby, but not Mother. Steven and I were not close; never had been, really. I always assumed, despite my efforts to cover-up the truth, that early-on he suspected I was gay and was ashamed of it. He did not want a gay brother. To have been brought into this world by the same mother, having nurtured us from her bosom, we were more like strangers, more foes than friends growing up. From the beginning, our paths lay in opposing directions. Somewhere early on, our link was severed, perhaps by the violence that rained down on us by our father. Steven was tougher, while I was more sensitive. He had the force of a lion within, while I

49

had the softness of the lamb. When we were little, our mother used to dress us like cowboys in matching red vests and chaps with white fringe. Even Sandra was included in the dress-up play with a red cowgirl skirt. We all had black boots and red hats. The three of us were the posse, riding off into the sunset on our bikes—our pretend trusty steeds; Sandra's with training wheels. Then, one day, we stopped playing together. We just stopped and never road off into the sunset again.

His was a success story. A self-made man, after dropping out of high school shortly after our father's suicide. The dishwasher and short-order cook at Shoney's became a very flourishing restaurant entrepreneur with several franchises. Most of our communications over the years had to do with our mother's, as well as some of our sister's, issues. After I moved to Atlanta, I tried to keep in contact with him and his family, but there was no reciprocation. I got the message after awhile, subtle as it was— stay away. It became obvious to me that he wanted to keep the past—his alcoholic, abusive father, the suicide, his crazy, alcoholic mother and gay brother—under the radar.

Debra got married a few years before our mother's illness. It was a huge wedding with three hundred guests— an outdoor extravaganza. Astonishingly, I did receive an invitation, but declined, much to my mother's disapproval.

"I'm not going if you don't go. You have to go!" she practically yelled at me.

"Mother, Debra is twenty-six and I've seen her only a few times in her life. I understand they come to Atlanta all the time...and not once did she look me up. Not once!"

"You have to go! I'll be very upset if you don't."

"Mother, you'll be fine. I'm not going...I'm a stranger

to her. She could care less if I'm there or not, and would probably prefer I didn't attend. I'm flabbergasted I got the invitation in the first place," I made my case.

What I did not tell my mother was that I was not going to be the "token gay uncle." After all, we still lived in the South.

There was another reason I was not attending the wedding besides the gay thing and Debra being old enough to reach out to me. I did not want to be around if my sister or mother made a scene of some sort in front of all the guests. Sandra had been very jealous of my brother's two girls. They were given everything she never had. There had been trouble before, and a wedding was the perfect place to make a scene. After a few-too-many drinks, there was no telling what bad feelings might rise up. With both Mother and Sandra there, the odds were doubled—double trouble.

I called my brother as soon as I got into the Rover, my heartbeats accelerated by my enduring rage. His voicemail picked up.

"What's this bullshit of you being a grandfather and not telling our mother? You're a fucking asshole. Asshole! How could you keep such a thing as important as a great-grandchild from her?" I yelled as my whole body shook.

I drove as fast as I could to the hospital, not fully stopping at the stop signs and running a red light. Two minutes later my brother called back.

"No one calls me an asshole, you shit," Steven yelled.

I reiterated what I had left on his voicemail and hung up before he could speak another word. My rage continued; years and years of it had been building up inside. He had never been a brother to me or a very good son to our mother. I do not ever remember him and his wife inviting

Mother to their home. Not once that I can remember hearing of! Not even for Thanksgiving or Christmas. He did just what he had to, to make it appear that he cared.

By the time I pulled into the hospital parking lot, it was getting dark. A car's tires squealed, turning a corner as I stepped onto the pavement. I turned my head to see my brother's new black Mercedes 550 pulling in two rows back. I zigzagged toward the front entrance through the maze of parked cars. As I reached the exterior stairs, I heard his car door slam. I could see the silhouette of his large frame trying to catch up with me. He angrily called out my name, but I kept going. I raced through the front doors of the Warner Robins Medical Center. Luckily, one of the elevator doors opened at my approach. An elderly woman and a nurse exited as I entered. Steven was just ten feet behind me and gaining. Thirty years ago he would have been able to catch me, but decades of smoking and overeating had slowed him down significantly. He used to be an athlete: football, basketball, baseball, you name it; he played it. The door closed and I was safe for the moment.

Mother was in the ICU on the third floor. I quickly reached for the phone outside the electric doors to gain entrance. I recognized Tracy's voice, one of the nurses who had been attending to Mother for the past few days. I thought she was very pretty and sweet. I got the feeling she liked me. It could have just been my imagination, but, still, I think she did. In another life, I thought, when I come back straight.

By the time I walked into my mother's room, Steven was a few steps behind. I had barely enough time to turn around before he was in my face—nose to nose.

"No one calls me an asshole," he said.

"I did," I said, just above a whisper.

"Well, at least I'm not a butt fucker," he said, the first time I can remember him ever giving reference to me being gay.

Steven was so close I could smell his breath. I remember thinking he must have had something Italian for dinner. His eyes were bulging and his face red from his exertion of trying to catch me.

Butt fucker! Oh no you didn't....You know nothing about me and certainly not enough to call me that, I thought to myself.

"I'm not ten-years-old. I'm not afraid of you anymore," I said, my teeth tightly clenched together, trying to keep my voice low and wondering if our mother could hear anything while in a coma.

I was scared, but not of him. I was scared of how messed up our family was and, at fifty-one-years-old, my older brother was in my face like we were dirty-faced children fighting on the playground over a toy, and our mother was in the hospital bed two feet from where we were standing with a breathing tube down her throat, a heart monitor and a half-dozen needles in her arms hooked up to IV machines.

Luckily, Tracy had seen Steven rushing in, and overheard him heatedly raising his voice at me. Well, my secret is out, I thought.

"Is something wrong?" She asked, from the doorway.

Steven took a step back. His demeanor suddenly rotated to that of uncomfortable and embarrassment.

"Yes, he needs to leave, or you need to call security," I said, as I walked over and stood closer to Mother's bed.

Steven turned around and walked out the door, not uttering another word.

53

"I'm sorry, Tracy."

"Family; you can't pick them," she smiled.

"Very true."

"Well, let me know if you need anything."

"Thanks, I will."

I picked up the stuffed toy cat from the windowsill and placed it on Mother's chest.

"Denny is missing you, Mother. You need to get better so you can go home and she'll stop looking for you."

I sat down in the chair next to her bed.

The next day, Rachel brought the grandchildren to Mother's hospital room. It was too late. It may have eased their guilt, but Mother had been waiting on them to come see her for the last two years of her life.

The Funeral

I continued to be captivated by the pictures of my mother
slowly flashing on the big, high-tech television. Although
I had seen them many times before, especially over the
previous days, she was now bigger than life and her loss
was suddenly magnified to the millionth degree. She had
finally made it to the big screen. What a waste, I thought
to myself. What a wasted life. The pictures were in order
of the years of her existence or, more fittingly, her survival: a little girl with a smudge of dirt from the farm on
her face, growing into a beautiful young woman, into a
wife, into motherhood, then into the years of torment—the
abuse, the death of her husband and the slothful drowning
into the bottom of a bottle, and, finally, into the depths of
uncertainty, depression and into periods of insanity. All

hidden behind the restrained smiles and calm façade on her face in image after image. But I knew, as each picture flashed, the truth of her ordeal concealed under her skin.

The funeral home began filling up with people. Crowds had always made me jumpy and uncomfortable. My nerves, combined with lack of sleep, were beginning to rise up from that deep place inside of me where insecurity lives. I wondered if I was going to be able to make it through the day. I hated speaking in public, even after all my book readings, I always felt a wave of nausea before each one. But someone had to get up and tell the truth. I could not leave it up to my sister or brother. I could not let our mother's life go unnoticed and the truths buried with her body. I pulled the folded papers out of my jacket pocket and, for the hundredth time, read over what I had written to be sure I had put down all I wanted to say—all that needed to be told. Soon, an audience of her friends and neighbors would be sitting in front of me, and I had to stand up for her. I had to tell the good and the bad. I knew this speaking engagement would be the most important one of my life!

I looked up from the rumpled pages in my hands to see Rachel's tall, well-dressed frame across the room. Debra was standing next to her. She was a pretty, full-figured girl with a round face and deeply set eyes. Her long dark brown hair was pulled back in a ponytail. I wondered where the baby was—my mother's great-grandchild. I assumed the other girl with her back toward me was Alice, the younger daughter. I was still angry they had waited to visit Mother until she was in a coma and was appalled that they had showed up, now. What was the point, I thought to myself? They did not seem to care about her in life, so why care now that she was gone? I tried to focus my attention on the true mourners who were there because they loved my mother. Their lives had been touched in one way or another by her.

Then, I saw faithful Siggy. She had always "been there" for my mother. JoAnn was standing beside her as they both stood in front of Mother's coffin. Siggy touched Mother's face. They had both fallen in love with Mother's spirit and quirky sense of humor. They were able to see past her drinking, and many times had unwaveringly tried to pull Mother out of her periods of depression. They both carried the bouquets of roses that Sandra was giving out at the entrance. For a moment my anger left me as I looked around and saw the friends and neighbors who would truly miss my mother.

Among them, I was relieved to see that Theodora and her long-time partner Hugh had arrived from Atlanta. I got up from my seat and walked over to them. She had always been a true friend. Theo, as I often called her, immediately saw my anxiety dripping off my forehead like sweat.

"Hello, Darling. How are you holding up?" she greeted, with open arms and a smile of concern on her face.

Hugh patted me on the back.

"I'm fine. So happy to see you, both," I said, trying not to burst out in tears.

"Well, I know you're happy to see us, Darling. But, you're not fine."

True to form, Theo could see right through to my very core. She had an instinct like that.

I had called her the afternoon before to read the eulogy I had written. Theo had always read everything I had written. She also knew how much I hated talking to groups.

"Darling, you'll be fine. The tribute you wrote for your mother is wonderful."

"I just want people to understand her," I said.

"I know, Darling. They will after you're finished."

"The grandchildren are here. I'm in shock," I told her.

"No shit?"

Theo knew the whole story about the grandchildren not making any attempt to contact Mother during her long illness and about the great-grandchild.

"I can't look them straight in the face. I'm afraid if I do I'll go off on them."

Theo reached in her purse and discreetly pulled out a prescription bottle.

"Here, fifteen minutes before you get up to speak, go to the bathroom and take half of this pill."

"What is it?"

"It's something to take the edge off. Take this and you'll be fine."

"You think it'll work? I just don't want to get up there and start crying."

"It will. It's magic. I have to pop one every time I'm around my relatives," Theo said, and then she winked at me.

"Thanks. Thanks again, both of you, for being here."

"We love you and are here for you. Don't forget."

"It means everything to me."

Soon the funeral hall was at capacity. I was comforted by seeing so many people had showed up for Mother, many scattered loosely around in groups. Sandra was talking nonstop to some of the neighbors. I only recognized a half-dozen faces, the rest were strangers. A good number of those in attendance were watching the pictures of Mother on the screen. Steven and his son were talking in another group in the large entry area; I assumed friends, employees and business associates, not there for our mother but for him. My eyes focused back on Rachel and her daughters. Alice still had her back to me. Her hair was full, dark and long. Suddenly, she turned around slightly to say something to her sister. I could see her profile. She looked bored. All of them: my brother, his wife and their children looked like they would rather be somewhere else. So did I, but for different reasons.

Rachel and the girls started to walk through the large archway into the adjoining room where my mother's body was on view. I still could not see all of Alice's face; her long, below-the-shoulder hair fell forward as she followed her mother and sister. I watched her walk past Mother's open casket as she barely glanced into it, perhaps overcome by guilt and too afraid to stop and look at the body of her grandmother; too afraid to face her even in death. She, as her mother and sister, moved hastily past the casket, her head down. I continued to watch, my eyes focused like a hungry house cat watching a mouse at a distance scurrying across the room. Then, she turned and looked in my direction; her face finally clearly in view from where I was standing. I looked up at the large flat screen, at the pictures of my mother when she was the same age as Alice. Suddenly, my anger subsided, pushed over by a feeling of mystification, and I become mesmerized. She had inherited my mother's unmistakable beauty. I looked at Alice again. I had to be sure I was not in some kind of confusion, my vision blurred by the lack of sleep and watery eyes. Then a feeling of astonishment ran through me. Their likeness was uncanny. Truly, she was the embodiment of her grandmother, as if time had suddenly reversed and she had walked right out of the over-sized flat screen. At that realization, a peace came over me. I understood and felt as if my mother had another chance at life through

Alice. I watched her until she became lost in the mix with the true mourners. Yes, the true mourners.

I checked my watch. The time was growing close. My nervousness—derailed temporarily by Alice—surfaced again. Within minutes I would have to stand in front of all these people, including my family, and talk about my mother's life. I knew I had to tell the truth and not sugar-coat it. I wanted them to understand her as I did. I wanted the grandchildren to understand the heartache they had caused their grandmother by not coming to see her. I wanted my brother to understand how wrong he was for not telling Mother about Debra's baby. And I wanted Debra to know she had wronged Mother just as much.

I slipped down a hallway and into the bathroom. A gust of warm air washed over me as the door closed. I stood in front of the large mirror, seeing my mother's eyes looking back at me. I searched my pant's pocket for the little pill from Theo. I bit it in half, swallowed and washed the other down the sink. I hope a half is enough, I thought to myself. I pulled two paper towels from the dispenser and ran the cool water running in the sink over them. Then I tried to wipe the apprehension off my face.

I took my seat in the front row, between my sister and brother. My aunt and uncle sat at the end toward the aisle. Steven's wife and children were in the row behind. I was still angry they were there. The day before, my uncle had cautioned me concerning what I was going to say at the service about my brother and his family; fretful I would cause some trouble. I promised I would not make a scene, even though that is what we had always done in this family: make a scene. One of my sister's childhood friends, Sherry, stood on the stage singing *God is Calling You*

Home accompanied by piano as the guests took their seats. Two other childhood friends, sisters—Carol and Cheryl— tenderly smiled from across the aisle. We always called Carol "freckled lip" because of the big freckle on her lower lip. As children, we ate plums off the huge tree in their back yard until we all got stomach-aches; and once played spin-the-bottle in the carport. Carol was the first girl I ever kissed.

Pastor Ellison started the sermon. I tuned him out. I wanted my mother to be around for another Thanksgiving and Christmas. The hard reality that the next day was Thanksgiving barreled its way into my head—a time when families gather to be together. The irony was killing me. This was the first one we had all been together since becoming adults. I wanted to make the up-coming holidays the best Mother had ever had, but I felt God had let me down. In truth, I felt I was the one who let my mother down. I had never prayed harder in my life after she went into the coma. I called everyone I could think of who went to church, asking them to request their congregation to pray for my mother, to pray for a miracle that she would come out of the coma.

Sandra followed Pastor Ellison. She looked very pretty, having really pulled herself together and fixed herself up. I could see a bit of Mother in her as she read a tender letter she had written to her. By then, the stinging raw emotions from the recent fight had been callused. Sandra's voice cracked and the tears began to flow from her eyes, but she managed to finish. My uncle got up and spoke lovingly about his big sister. Originally, he did not want to speak, but, earlier that morning, he gave in to some arm twisting on my part. He spoke eloquently about her as a girl with big eyes eager to learn and then developing, later, into a beautiful young woman. Then it was my turn. I felt surprisingly calm. Theo's magic pill seemed to be working. I just did not want to cry in front of everyone, especially my brother and his family.

I stood up from my seat, took a deep breath of courage before taking the five steps forward. I counted them to myself: one, two, three, four, five as I took each one. I took a second, cavernous breath, before taking the four steps up to the stage. At the top, I turned around, looking out over the full room through a thin layer of tears skinning my eyes; tears that I was determined not to allow to fall out of my sockets. I pulled the well-worn pages from my jacket and placed them on the podium. I began ... *My mother was a woman with great potential and promise, a woman full of dreams. Somewhere along the way she lost herself. I want you to know who my mother is, not was. For although she has left this place to begin a new journey, she will forever be a part of this world by the very fact she lived as a mortal. I want you to know how much I will miss her physical presence. But, I know she will always be in my heart, and walking beside me as I make it through the trying days ahead, as well as holding me dearly, as only a mother can do.*

I stumbled over a few words, forced to pause for a moment as my throat began to close up. The audience was totally quiet waiting to hear what I was going to say next; waiting to see if I was going to keep my composure or breakdown. I looked back up and out over the crowd again. My eyes were still wet and heavy; it appeared I was standing looking through a pool of water. But I could see Theo, in her wide-brim hat, smiling at me, giving me the thumbs up. And there was Neil, another friend from Atlanta, in the row behind, giving me encouragement to go on with a slight smile and a nod of his head.

I cleared my throat and continued … *As a mortal, my Mother was beautiful—both inside and out—with a tender, loving heart. She was also a contradiction. Mother has a spirit like no other—strong, but fragile—determined, but vacillating—sweet, but feisty. And that spirit is still with us.*

Sadly, as much as she was beautiful, she was troubled. The best way to describe her is as a survivor and as someone who held on to hope at all cost. For many years, she struggled with mental distresses, an abusive husband, his alcoholism, as well as that of her own, and his suicide while she was just rooms away as he shot himself. I truly believe that in the beginning they had a great love—as passionate as it was unpredictable, but it later turned turbulent and eventually fell into chaos. Today, I know she has forgiven him. It is because of those things Mother never realized just how beautiful she was, and she never realized her potential. Yes, I would call her a survivor. All these factors left her misunderstood and abandoned by some. Where others would have totally given up, she pushed on and tried—tried to find the good things in life and some happiness.

I paused to push back my emotions before speaking about the things she loved about life:

> *She loved to dance and sing.*
> *She loved collecting sheet music.*
> *As a young girl, she loved to write to movie stars, and cherished two encounters with one of her favorites, Gene Autry, who saw her potential even if she did not see it in herself.*
> *She loved to read.*

She loved mysteries, both in books and movies.
Mother loved her pets—3 cats: Denny, Emmy, and
Donnie— and her crazy run-a-way dog, Suzie.
And, of course, Sandra's dog, Dallas.
She loved CNN and was Nancy Grace's biggest
fan. Nancy corresponded some with mother, and
even called her during one of her last stays in the
hospital.
She loved Anne Murray and her songs.
And Chanel No. 5.

I took another breath of courage and swallowed it.

These are the things that I will remember and will miss
about her:
Me, as a young boy, following her around while
holding onto her skirt. I even got lost in it a few
times.
Her singing and humming around the house in
happier days.
Her Divinity and Alaskan cookies, and German
Chocolate cakes.
Her taking me from my bed at night, so she could
hold me while she watched television and old mov-
ies, or just to sit by the radio singing along to the
songs she loved.
Her rubbing my legs at night for hours— in my
early teen years—as she soothed away the grow-
ing pains in them so I could fall asleep.
The very fact she believed in me when I did not
believe in myself. While I was still in high school,
she entered some of my art in a contest at the mall
without telling me. Shortly after, she presented me

with the prize ribbon my work had won.
*Our late nights together, as she helped me write
my college papers, because God knows, with my
dyslexia, I could not spell worth a crap, and my
punctuation was enough to make the best of edi-
tors run screaming from the room. It is because of
my mother I am a writer today.*
*Her telling me always to watch out for those big
trucks on the highway on my trips back and forth
to visit. Now, she will be watching out for them for
me on every road trip I take.*
*For caring enough to make sure she had my favor-
ite things to eat on those visits.*
*The look in her eyes when she opened the door
that told me, without words, that she loved me.*
Her generosity.
Birthday cards.
Thanksgivings.
*And, those damn socks and underwear every
Christmas.*
*The way she could make me feel like I was ten
years old again—which could be a good or a bad
thing, depending on the situation.*
*Her phone calls—the ones where she talked and
talked on and on—that, many times drove me
crazy. I long for those phone calls again.*
*And, how hard it was for me to leave her every
time I had to drive back to Atlanta. Sometimes, I
would make excuses just to come back to give her
another kiss before pulling out of the driveway. I
remember often driving around the block and coming back.*
Mother always telling me to dye my graying hair,

because she did not want it to give HER age away.
Her smile, that left a warm feeling in my heart.
Her laugh, although rare in later years, that I
wanted to hear more of.
The expression on her face—when she opened a
present—that exploded with joy no matter how big
or small the gift.
By the last three kisses I gave her, one-after-the-
other on her cheek, the last time she was able to
speak to me, and the ones she gave me in return.
And, there are so very many more…

Then I looked at my brother, his wife and their children and spoke about what Mother left on this earth:

From her womb, she gave life to three children.
And from one of those lives, Steven's, there came
three grandchildren and a great-grandchild. I
wanted to say—*of which she never knew existed*
and was never given the chance to hold in her
*arms, but she knows now—b*ut I resisted.
A big hole in my heart, left by her passing, that in
time will be filled again by her loving spirit.

Satisfied, I folded the papers and put them back in my pocket as I looked over the crowd. The grandchildren were crying with their heads down. I wondered if they had finally realized what they had stolen from my mother and what they had missed. I wondered if my brother had any regret. Most of all, I wondered if Debra, her eyes red and tear-filled—now being a mother herself—realized how she would feel if her own daughter did what she had done to her grandmother one day. One day she may find out.

I returned to my seat. Sherry sang another song. The Pastor said a closing prayer. When he finished, one of the funeral directors motioned for my family to follow him back up the aisle. Everyone stood and watched Mary Ellen's family exit the hall. Some family. She deserved better, I thought.

Theo ran up to me with open arms. Her hug was life giving; it was what I needed at that moment.

"You did an excellent job. Your mother would be proud of you, Randy. She is proud of you," Theo corrected.

Siggy hugged me next, then JoAnn, as Carol and Cheryl approached.

"If my two children do for me what you just did for your mother, I'll be happy," Cheryl said.

For a moment I wished I could go back to when we were all kids eating the big, ripe plums off the tree in Carol and Cheryl's backyard. I had a different stomachache now.

Uncle Ben and Aunt Jerry said their goodbyes. They were heading back to Fayette.

After the service, the funeral director informed us they would not be departing for Columbus, Georgia, for another hour. There Mother's body would be laid to rest on top of our father's. Someone suggested lunch at my brother's restaurant. I cringed at the thought, not wanting to be forced to speak to his family, much less share a meal, but it would be a scene if I had refused and chose to sit in the car while the rest of them ate. I did not have a stomach for food or for my brother and his family. A family that neither I, nor my mother and sister, for that matter, were ever invited to be a part of.

I felt like a little boy—small and helpless—as I sat at the end of the table watching the restaurant filling up with lunchtime appetites. My suit was uncomfortable on my body; feeling foreign. It had been years since I had worn one. My older brother sat at the other end glancing over the menu he was very well familiar with, since he was the owner, refusing to look me in my eyes; still red and watery from the morning's event. Even at the service, he would not look at me while I was standing at the podium giving our mother's eulogy. I wanted him to cry as I had. I wanted to see his tears run down his face, but he never showed any emotion, any regret related to the loss of our mother. I saw nothing on his face; not a trace of tenderness crossed his seemingly unbreakable exterior. Perhaps in his moments of solitude during her long illness and after her passing he cried in his car, or in the backyard of his house, or in the bathroom, or perhaps he sat on the edge of her hospital bed when no one was around and cried. But, I never saw a tear drop from his stone eyes. Then I wondered if he remembered how mother's hands were stained for days after she dyed his good shoes black for his junior/senior dance. If he remembered all the little things she did for him, as well as the big.

Rachel sat next to him. They seemed estranged, not acknowledging each other's presence at the table. Sandra was to her right. Across from her was Debra. Next to her sat Carl. Then there was Alice, the one I could not keep my eyes off from the moment she turned toward me at the funeral home. We were all sitting around the lunch table at Cheddars, a family style restaurant, looking over the menus like nothing had happened, while back at the funeral home our mother was being loaded into the back of a black hearse. No one said a word about the service. Not a single word. Nor did they reminisce about Mother's life. The two girls talked about clothes and who they thought was the hottest new Hollywood celebrity. Carl was quiet while Sandra talked with Rachel. Steven got up from the table to check on something in the restaurant; an excuse, I am sure just to separate himself even more. So, I sat there looking at them, searching for some connection and feeling none, except for the single irrefutable fact: the woman in the coffin had given us life.

After lunch, I was dumbfounded that Rachel and the children were going to make the drive to Columbus. I had assumed that only Steven, Sandra and I would be going. They were willing to drive two and a half hours to watch their grandmother being lowered into the ground, but over the last two years, they could not drive twenty minutes across town to visit her while she was sick.

Sandra came with me in the Rover. Steven and Carl drove in my brother's Mercedes, while the girls and their mother followed in her Lexus. We were anything but a family in three cars following at a guarded distance, as we had in life, signifying just how separate our lives were.

The sad irony is that, on the day of Mary Ellen's funeral, the very day her body was lowered into the ground, the great-grandchild she never knew existed and never got to hold, turned one-year-old.

Two weeks later, after we settled our mother's estate and sold the house, I helped my sister move to San Antonio, Texas. Sandra had been stationed there years ago for a period of time when she was in the Army. She wanted to go back to live with a good friend. She drove to Atlanta with her BMW solidly packed, including her dog, Dallas, and Mother's favorite cat, Denny. Sandra found new homes for the other two cats and Suzie. We left Atlanta the next morning before dawn to drive to Columbus to pay our respects to Mother, then on to Tuscaloosa, Alabama, to take Mother's treasured pearl necklace to her Aunt Anne, and then on to Texas. Denny meowed the whole way until we finally arrived the next morning by ten o'clock. I flew back to Atlanta the following morning.

Chain-link Fencing

The hospital towered on the rolling hillside over the parking lot. The massive, anomalous light blue building had a central structure with two thinner buildings, on either side, jetting out from it like bricked wings. The one to the right had a large terrace off the top floor completely enclosed with chain-link fencing up to the rooftop. Only the windows on the upper two floors on that side were covered in the same manner. It looked like a prison, and somehow I knew the chain-link was there to keep everyone inside, separating them from the outside world.

It was 1964, and I was nine-years-old. We were living in Columbus, Georgia. Our father left us in the car while he went up to see our mother. He had been gone for an hour or more. My sister, brother and I sat in the station wagon, waiting. Sandra and I in the back seat, while Steven was in the rear laying out flat on his back staring at the sagging fabric lining of the roof. Toys and pieces of a board game were scattered all around the seats, floorboard and back of the wagon, but we were not interested in playing children's games, being rather preoccupied with the seriousness of the moment and why we were closed up in the car on such a nice, sunny Saturday and not romping in our backyard like children our age were supposed to. We did not speak a word amongst ourselves as we breathed air in and uncertainty out. The periods of complete silence were interrupted by infrequent noises from the surrounding parking lot: people talking as they walked to and from their cars; hurried footsteps; keys jangling; car doors opening and closing; engines stopping and starting up; and the siren of an ambulance returning to the hospital's emergency room entrance. Even at nine, I had that feeling of disquiet in my belly. It was not the first time we had been told to stay in the car, and it would not be the last. We were told Mother was sick again and in this place to get well.

Another wait had finally ended when we heard the march of our father's heavy footsteps, distinguishable from the others, approaching on the asphalt. The back door opened. Our father stood stiffly in the parking lot. All I could see of him was from his waist down. He was wearing his Army fatigues. His boots were black and exceedingly shiny. The buckle of his belt reflected the light like a mirror into my eyes.

"Get out and wave at your mother," he instructed, like we were soldiers in his platoon.

"Is she coming home?" my sister asked.

"No," he answered, in a strict voice that really meant hurry up.

Chain-link Fencing

My brother climbed over the seat, exiting first, followed by Sandra, and then I slid across and out of the car. We stood side by side against the two-toned beige and green Buick as our father towered over us. His impenetrable black hair was cut in a flat-top, as rigid as he was standing. He stared at us with deep blue-set eyes that showed little emotion, pointing his hand in the direction of the bricked building's upper floors with the chain-link fencing. We looked up like lost children trying to find our way home. A rogue breeze kicked up in the extremely, bright Fall day, sweeping my sister's long blond hair into my face, stinging my eyes and obscuring the view.

As the breeze weakened, I could see a woman standing on the terrace, her body limply pressed against the fencing; her fingers sticking out grabbing a tight hold of the diamond-shaped wires. There were other patients marauding around like caged animals in the background. She seemed so far away, out of reach of our short extended arms. Mother looked small, like one of my sister's dolls, dressed in a long, pale-colored gown as she called out to us, "I love you," but her faint words were carried off in the wind before they could reach our little ears. The only feelings I had at that moment were heartbreak and confusion as I stood there on that day looking at my mother imprisoned on the top floor of the threatening building, uncertain why we were unable to go up with our father to see her, to hug her. I was convinced he was keeping us from our mother. I was also feeling resentment toward him. As any child would, I missed my mother, and I knew he had played a part in putting her there.

During my childhood my mother had been hospitalized many times for depression and fits of rage. That time, she was carried from the house on a stretcher, kicking and screaming, as two paramedics tried to control her, strapping her down with wide, thick cotton wrist restraints, and longer ones across her violently squirming body. My sister, brother and I watched as they rolled her out of the house and over the bumpy driveway. I felt helpless as her eyes darted back and forth, her screams going unanswered. Then, she looked pensively at me as the men were about to slide her into the back of the ambulance, and I somehow felt her pain. That day has never left me. The day they took her away and she shared her deepest, darkest pain with me as by some form of transference as our eyes met and locked for a brief second.

On numerous occasions, during various stays in the hospital, she was given electro convulsive therapy, commonly referred to as shock treatments. They were supposed to help severely depressed patients, when psychotherapy and medication seemed to be ineffective in their recovery. She would be away for days or weeks at a time. Then, my father would bring her home from the hospital. She would hug each one of us and then go to bed. Usually, the next day, Mother was properly dressed and had make-up on; her hair perfectly styled as if she had been to the beauty parlor just hours before. She was busy making breakfast, packing our lunches and seeing us off to school. It was miraculous. She would seem to be on her way to recovery and her old self would appear. The days to follow, the house would be filled with sweet aromas of Mother's baked German-chocolate cake, Alaskan cookies, and divinity fudge, and the house would be clean from floor to ceiling. There was a thread of hope again that the dark times were behind us. But it was just a thin thread, because that hope had been broken before.

That hope would last days, weeks, sometimes months,

and then Mother would begin to slip away—and then eventually disappear into—some subterranean, dark place inside of her. She would tell us she was sorry and would try harder before going back to bed. "Tomorrow, I'll be okay," she would say. But usually "tomorrow" she was not. She would still try to take care of us, but without the make-up or beauty parlor hair. She did not dress, instead wore her housecoat all day. When we left for school she would go back to bed, staying there until we returned home.

My father had no patience for what he believed was Mother's instability. The fact that he was not stable, as well, did not help. Soon, after she began to decline again, he would show his rage. He would begin to drink, and the more he did, the more it showed. The frustration grew on my father's face like he was going through a metamorphosis. The muscles under the skin of his forearms would protrude, his fingers closed tightly into the palms of his hands while the veins at his temples would pop and pulsate. It was worse on his days off from work. We avoided him like mice do the house cat.

It was one early summer; school had just let out a few days before. When most kids were excited about the long break ahead, I was on edge. Like it was yesterday, I remember the June sky was a baby-blue and dotted with high popcorn-shaped clouds. My sister, brother and I were outside in the backyard in ankle-high grass filled with dandelions. Sandra was digging a hole in a patch of dirt, using an old tablespoon with a bent handle for a shovel, filling a yellow plastic bucket that had a crack up the side. Steven was halfway up the only tree in the yard. I was walking along the fence with a stick when our individual play and the thumping of the stick were interrupted by our father's yelling at our mother, "Stop being crazy. You're just lazy! You're useless! Go wash the dishes."

Their bedroom faced the backyard. We had a clear view from the open, double window. It was a hot day in the un-air-conditioned house. A fan was propped up in one of the windows. Father was visible through the other, standing over the bed shirtless, wearing a pair of pants. The veins in his forearms were prominent. His biceps engorged with blood as his muscular arms waved over our mother propped up in the bed.

"I'll get up in a minute."

"No. You'll get up now."

My father then lunged at her, physically pulling her out of bed. He held her up like she was a rag doll and forced her to the kitchen, continuing his yelling.

I ran to the back door unnoticed. My sister continued her digging and filling the bucket. My brother jumped out of the tree and ran over. He stopped in his tracks behind me. We watched our mother standing on the linoleum floor in her bare feet, shaking at the kitchen sink, looking at the stack of dirty breakfast dishes. Our father stood next to her, unrelenting, giving out orders like she was a Private in his Army. After a few moments she raised her hand to comb the hair out of her face, and then reached for the faucet handle.

As soon as my father left the house for work, Mother would return to her bedroom to find sanctuary from the darkness inside of her. She would stay there until she heard his car pull in the driveway. Then, she would get out of bed and start making dinner, still in her housecoat, still in that deep, dark hole. As a matter of course, on entering the house, Father would get a beer from the refrigerator and head for the living room where he would sit in his lounge chair in front of the television. One beer became two, then three, then four. The more he drank, the meaner he became. He seemed compassionless at times. He would then lash out, striking her if she said or did something of which he did not approve. After such episodes, my mother would be up the next morning, in her house coat, trying. Battered, sometimes with a black-eye, but trying and believing it was her fault.

At night, when she put me to bed, I could see the pain in her brown eyes as she held my head in her hands.

"Don't worry, Darling, things will get better. I'll try. I'll get better," she would say.

Sometimes late at night, when my father was away on assignment, and my sister and brother were fast asleep, she would pick me up out of my bed and carry me to the living room. Mother would rock me in her arms while watching old movies on the television, or sit in the dark listening to music on the radio or playing records, softly singing to me, singing along to the songs she favored by Billie Holiday, Vera Lynn, Judy Garland, Frank Sinatra, Perry Como and others—reliving her dreams of becoming a singer in her younger years. Her voice was engaging with a hint of sadness as she sang like a caged bird. It soon became evident to me that she did not need chain-link fencing to separate her from the world. Something had happened to her long before she married my father and long before his abuse. I know now that there was something deep inside of her that was her prison. It was not made of wire, stone or mortar, but of a series of events that left her isolated from the world she so much wanted to be a part of—as a heavy rain fell inside of her.

Going Home

For years, I had never felt a connection with Fayette, Alabama, the place I experienced my first breaths of life. Even as a child, on family visits back to this quiet place of faintly rolling hills and subtle curves in the roads, I felt a contradiction of emotions toward this birthplace I shared with my mother. On one hand, there was an eerie strangeness hovering in the air and, on the other, there was a sense of beginning, and in that, a minute level of comfort. It was the place my mother kept coming back to no matter how unhappy it made her, and wherever my mother was—was home for me.

Many of my memories are as hazy as the morning fog that creeps low and copiously through the cotton fields in the premature hours before the sun marks the horizon of a new day. Then, there are others that are as clear as the pristine water that runs in-between and over the rocks along the stream ambling on the other side of the road I walked hand and hand with my mother on a hot summer's afternoon; our shoes crunching into the dirt, the sharp edges of the gravel pushing up into their soles, as a round, fiery sun tanned the pale skin of our winter flesh. Surrounded by what felt like an endless openness of fields, pastures, and winding dirt roads, we listened to the concert of the hum of summer, muffled by its silent, still heat: the incessant high pitch cries of katydids, hiding in the tall, dry grass; the soft, murmuring calls of the mating doves of June filling the air; the sound of the flowing water in the background—calm and steady—following the bend of the road. All consistent, grounding us to the earth. And the sweet humming of my mother's voice mixed-in as she daydreamed.

We walked where the road took us, aimlessly, until our feet tired and our thirst required a visit back to the well to refresh ourselves with the cavernous, cool water it offered. Even then, she was a different woman. There was still promise in her eyes and a world of possibilities running around in her mind and heart.

"Fayette was never intended to be your birthplace," she told me on one of those early walks, as if to offer me an apology for bringing me into the world in the place she tried so hard to escape.

My mother had been in France with my father, my older brother, and me eight months in her belly. Steven was just getting over a bout of pneumonia and our mother thought it best to get him back to America as soon as possible. Most of the preceding year he had been sick with colds and a constant runny nose due to the damp conditions in which they had been living. Although terrified of airplanes, pregnant and with a small, sickly child, she decided to fly back early. The Army was in the process of changing my father's duty station to Fort Benning in Georgia and, once he was reassigned, he would pick us up. The return flight was so rough, she thought she was going to give birth over the Atlantic Ocean. She did not board another plane for forty years. It would be cars, buses, or trains until then. The road that took her away had brought her back again.

On June 21, 1955, my mother opened a drawer of the dresser in her old bedroom, whereupon she was startled by a chicken snake that had set up housekeeping. They were notorious—the chicken snakes—for getting into the old farmhouse during the hot summer days. Apparently they were so bad that her mother would not allow any grass to grow around the house in hopes of keeping their invasion at a minimum. But one got in, and it was enough to send Mother into an early labor. I came into this world at 2:40 p.m., on a Tuesday, at the McNease & Robertson Hospital.

After our walks, we sat against the well, shaded by the long-reaching limbs of the all-knowing, old black walnut tree with its expansive, massive roots anchored profoundly into the ground. I remember one afternoon as if it was yesterday; my recollection as clear as the water we took to quench our thirst. My mother held the ladle up to my lips as I took a mouthful of the cool, invigorating water. Then she took what was left for herself. She laughed as she reached over to wipe the dripping water from my chin. My brother was in the garden, on the other side of the house, with our grandmother and Great-grandmother Rushing picking strawberries for a pie. Our sister had yet to be born. Grandfather was across the road hammering loose boards back into place on the side of the barn. The sounds of the impact of his forceful swings rang across the road.

It is one of those pristine memories, a snapshot pulled from the family photo album of a perfect moment when everything seemed at peace. But pictures do not always show what is going on deep inside of our souls. My mother appeared happy in the moment, but still longed to be somewhere else. Even then, I could see it in the distant stare of her eyes as she looked past the garden, beyond the dirt road and over the cotton fields that were just beginning to bud. Her dreams were still alive inside of her, trying to open like the cotton just a few feet away, but she found herself back where it all began, waiting to leave again.

"Son, I used to sit under this old tree when I was your age and pet my little dog," she told me.

"You had a dog?"

"A little black dog."

"Where is it now?"

"She went to heaven many years ago."

"Oh. What was her name?"

"Sadie. Sadie was her name."

I sat and listened to my mother tell me stories of a little girl as the shade of the walnut grew longer and longer, thinner and thinner, as the sun moved across the sky to the other side of the world.

After so many years, it was time to go back. Despite my resistance, this was a journey I had to make; to return to the place of our births. Over the years, when people inquired where I was from, my generic reply was: I was born in Fayette, Alabama, but never really lived there.

Their response was usually, "That's odd; you don't have a southern accent." The years of my father's violence had scarred-over the gentle memories of the time I spent there with my mother. I had convinced myself there were no ties there for me in the small, out-of-the-way place easily passed-by on the interstate heading west; in the middle of cotton and corn fields carved out of the tree-packed landscape. I had to go back to find those ties again; to find the connections and part of my mother's soul that she had left behind.

The night before the trip, I set my alarm for 3:30 a. m. Although I tried to sleep, I lay wide awake thinking about the four-hour drive ahead and what I was going to find once I arrived. I had not seen my Uncle Ben and Aunt Jerry since the funeral a year and one month ago, but bizarrely it seemed like it had been just days. Before that, maybe six times in fifty-two years, and I had not been back to Fayette since I was a freshman in college.

It was black and freezing outside my house as I dragged the dog crate to the Rover. The street light, parasitic and high on the telephone pole, emitted a murky, limited glow. Only the house on the corner, on the other side of the street, showed any sign of life by the light from a small window on the second floor. Other than that, the neighborhood appeared dead to the world. I opened the tailgate. The top section refused to stay up and kept sliding down before I could lift the dog crate into the back. I cursed myself for not having the struts replaced last winter. I gingerly rested the gate on my head while awkwardly sliding the crate inside. I threw my bag and a six-pack of Diet Cokes in the back seat. At 4:15 Dugan and I pulled out of the driveway. Luckily, he had quickly fallen back asleep in the crate. I wished I was still in bed, too.

By 5:45, and two Diet Cokes later, we had crossed the state line as the headlights raced across the sign: *Welcome to Alabama the Beautiful State.* The car's thermostat read 22 degrees outside. I cranked up the temperature dial to eighty. There was a blue-white chunky frost on the land in every direction I looked. In the dark, the icy blades of grass reflected what little light was around, making them appear to be sharp little knives sticking out of the ground. I heard Dugan stirring in his crate. I looked in the rearview mirror to see the back of his white head as he inquisitively watched one of the few cars trailing behind us. He made a low growl and then barked, before becoming distracted by his tail. Dugan started chasing it, quickly becoming an annoying habit. The crate rattled as his circular movement shook it. I wondered when he was going to grow out of chasing his tail and then smiled to myself. Calling out to him would be fruitless; he is deaf. One out of every five white, blue-eyed, English Bull Terriers is usually deaf. I got him as a gift for my boyfriend, but the dog stays with me most of the time, due to the fact that Christopher is still in college, thirty years younger, and another book to write in itself. But he told me he wanted the relationship and was willing to do whatever it took to make it work. I was skeptical at first, but soon found myself falling in love with him. So instead of finally moving to California, I stayed for love.

I referred to the Map Quest directions lying on the dashboard. I did not want to miss I-459 toward Montgomery and then I-359 to Tuscaloosa. I kept drifting into a fog thinking about my mother and her final days. I was concerned my reminiscing would cause me to pass the exit sign. I am horrible at following directions. Thirty minutes later, a low pink-orange light illuminated the horizon in the rear-view mirror. By the time I made it to my first exit, I could see the light growing as the sun chased me west. The temperature had climbed a degree and the frost was still holding on tightly to every surface outside except the road. I thought about keeping the Rover headed west, to California. Just keep going, I told myself. Keep going west like I had thought on countless junctures in my life. But I had fallen in love with Christopher and could never leave him behind, not even for California.

I had the radio on a morning talk show, *Alabama Morning*, I think, out of Birmingham; which I had bypassed a while back. The hosts were talking about the upcoming presidential election and the close battle between Clinton and Obama for the Democratic ticket. I thought how much my mother would have wanted to vote for Hilary Clinton. It would have made her proud to see a woman in the White House. The hosts switched their conversation to the weather. To my relief, the temperature was projected to reach 58. Good, I'll take that over 23 degrees any day, I thought to myself. I looked back at the rising sun in the rear-view mirror.

I turned on US-43, amazed at how beautiful that part of Alabama is; how still and reticent it appeared as the icy countryside reflected the low, tiptoeing light of the expanding sunlight. Perhaps I was overwhelmed and this journey had made me misty-eyed, taking my heart on a roller coaster ride filling up with regrets. My mother's regrets mostly; some mine. Or, was it just the time of the morning when everything was waking up from a cold night's sleep, as the sun's light caught up with me; easing over the rear of the Rover and steadily brightening up the sky in front of me?

85

For forty minutes I passed by old houses, some overgrown with vines, in the middle of open fields—all still covered in frost; horses and cattle grazing their breakfast, and old ramshackled fencing meant to keep them in. Concerned, I thought about checking my directions again. I believed I was on US-43, or at least I should be according to the directions. The last sign was thirty minutes behind me, and then, all of a sudden, a sign for US-82 raced pass. I thought that indeed my reminiscing had distracted me. I pulled the directions off the dashboard and slid my glasses, resting on my head, down to my eyes to see that there was no US-82 on the paper. That voice inside my head told me to pull over at the next gas station.

Dugan had fallen back into his puppy sleep. I did not see his head anymore. The motion of the car was soothing him. I thought what a lucky dog he is, even if he is deaf. Then my mind drifted to Christopher, imagining him still slumbering, his blond hair messy and those blue-green eyes that took my heart, soon to be stirring to get ready for class. I thought about the first time we kissed—of how nervous I was. I had waited a long time to find love—real love. From the corner of my eye, I spotted what looked like a mom-and-pop food mart and gas station just off the highway.

The cold air hit me as I stepped out of the Rover. Large clouds of breath exited and entered my nose and mouth as I walked to the entrance of the establishment. Behind the high counter a petite, elderly lady welcomed me with a smile as I came through the front door tightly gripping my directions. I smiled back with a look she probably had seen more times than her age. It was the look—I am lost.

"Hello, did you come in so I can help you get more

lost? You don't look like you're from around these parts," she said, with a sugary, Southern tone in her voice.

I laughed before asking her how to get to Fayette. She looked sweet, grandmotherly sweet. When she talked I could hear a slight whistle and a random delicate clicking caused by her dentures not fitting properly. I had not heard that whistle since being around my grandparents. She noticed my Rover parked at the front door.

"That's one of those fancy British vehicles. Don't see many of those around these here parts."

"It's old. Had it for a long time."

"Oh, Honey, bet it's not as old as me."

I laughed, again.

In a caring demeanor, she told me to turn around and go a mile or so to US-171 and go left. I looked down at my directions. I saw US-171 toward the bottom. I realized I had overshot and was heading in the wrong direction toward Columbus, Mississippi. Apparently I missed AL-18 in my reminiscing. I thought about getting a snack for the road. Then decided against it.

"Now, you be sure to be careful. That US-171 is deceiving and quickly gets very curvy once you turn off the main road. I hear those SUVs tip over easily."

I was amused and touched by her concern for my safety. I told her I would and thanked her for the directions and that concern before asking how long it will take. She told me thirty minutes, but reminded me to go slow— just like my mother would have.

Dugan was sitting up in the crate watching me as I returned to the Rover. The woman stood at the glass door looking out as I opened the tailgate. I was sure he had to pee, and carried him over to a grassy area. I could tell Dugan did not like the cold ground under his paws and he quickly took care of the business at hand. The lady scampered out of the store into the cold, tightly wrapping her quilted jacket around her body.

"What a cute puppy-dog. It's General Patton's dog, right?" she comments.

"Thank you. Yes, it is, and the RCA and the Target dog, too" I laughed, as I put Dugan back in his crate, while the lady was still admiring him.

I backed up the Rover and waved goodbye. She enthusiastically reciprocated. I reached for another Diet Coke, but stopped myself thinking four in three-and-a-half hours are too many, even for me.

I found US-171, like the woman had promised. The road started out straight at first, but, as she had warned, it quickly turned snake-like. It was not long before I began seeing familiar sights in the lay of the land. The snapshots, filed away in my mind years ago, were becoming alive. I remembered being a young boy in the back of my father's station wagon feeling motion sickness as he maneuvered the car over these same curves and hills, and raced by blurring fields of white.

For a road trip, my father's preference was to leave late in the night, my brother, sister and I dressed in our pajamas. My brother's and mine most likely printed in a cowboy theme, and my sister's in pink flowers. On the trips, my father would put a mattress in the back of the station wagon so we could sleep, but I typically stayed wide awake. As the car sped over the black top, I loved lying on my back, my head propped on a pillow pushed against the inside of the tailgate. I could see the back of my parents' heads. My mother's was typically compactly covered in hair rollers—the prickly kind that looked like bottle cleaners held in securely against her scalp with pink plastic pins—under a colorful scarf.

I would watch the variety of warping lights, from the signs of different business establishments, flying around their heads through the car's windshield and the side windows. They appeared like streaks of lights flashing and shooting into the car as if they were attached to arrows, bent and distorted by the slight curvature of the glass. I was able to tell if we were passing through a town or in a remote area by the speed of the car and the frequency and intensity of the light invasion. In the more out-of-the-way areas, the lights were few and far between. An isolated street lamp would flash and illuminate the interior of the car for a split second. Or, the overhead lights of a billboard, bursting with an advertisement, filled the car with distorted color and graphics for the blink of an eye. Then the car would slow down and an explosion of white and colored lights would begin their attack, and I knew we were cruising through one of the many small towns between Middle Georgia and Fayette, Alabama.

Our arrivals usually took place just after sun up. The electric lights faded as the darkness outside the car began to give way to a soft yellow-white glow from the rising sun. From the back of the station wagon, I watched my mother pull the scarf off her head and begin removing the rollers. Then she would pull out a hand mirror from her travel bag, wedging it in the windshield visor so she could comb out the perky curls and set them with Aqua Net hair spray. Random spurts of mist floated in the air around her head, filling the car with a sticky, sweet scent. My father would cough and comment, "Easy honey on the spray, you're going to fog us in." Once finished with styling her hair, Mother would apply her makeup for the day. I could see her reflection in the mirror. She was beautiful, simply beautiful to me.

Soon my father would pull the car off Highway 43 onto the dirt road. The smooth pavement ended as the car dipped onto the coarse terrain. The sound of whistling tires was replaced by the popping and crackling of the small rocks flying up from under the car like machine gun fire. Clouds of dust rose up completely covering the car by the time we made it the few more miles to my grandparents' house.

Suddenly I felt like I was getting close—close to something I had left behind. The landscape was beautiful in all its rural glory and I felt a peace about being alone on the road. The temperature had moved up to 38 degrees and much of the blue frost had lost its hold on the warming ground. Willingly I allowed the road to take me back. A few miles in, I slowed the Rover as I passed a cotton field picked clean except for a few scattered white balls, reminders of the generations of farmers that had lived here and worked the land as my grandfather had. I thought about the first time I had looked out the car window and seen the landscape covered in white, and for a second thinking it was snow. I saw my mother sitting in the front seat fixing her hair. Then, I wondered what she must have been thinking each time she made the journey home.

Fortunately, I gained an hour after I crossed the state line into the Central Time Zone. I wanted to get to Fayette as early as possible in order to have a full day. The closer I got, the more I felt like my mother was pulling me back; like she wanted me to know who she really was before she changed—before her dreams were shattered. The road continued to slither over the low, unassuming hills like a snake. It was all coming back to me.

At 7:47 I crossed the city limit sign: *Welcome to Fay-ette, Alabama Established 1821.* The small, sleepy town streets were unpopulated. The Rover was the only vehicle in sight. I pulled up to the side of the modest, two story, conventional wooden white house. After all these years, I had a faint memory of it. Dugan was up again looking at the new sights and ready to get out of his crate. I took him to my uncle's fenced-in backyard and coaxed him through the gate. He looked at me with a puzzled face, before running off to explore his surroundings. Within seconds, Dugan caught sight of an old discarded shoe, quickly capturing it and making it his own. I knew it would keep him occupied for a good part of the morning.

My uncle had heard the Rover and was waiting at the front door. I had never been close to him; perhaps partly my fault, but mostly due to a combination of things. As a child, I remember liking him, but then, I was looking for a better father. I liked most men who showed me any kind of attention or kindness. After my father killed himself, Mother and Uncle became estranged due to her frequent late-night phone calls, her voice thickly liquored and full of anger. It got to be too much for him and his family and, after awhile, they stopped answering the phone past a certain hour. But, during the last two years of her life, my uncle was there for her.

He was a religious man, so I was uncertain—as I had been of my mother—of how he would handle the knowledge that I was gay. So for years, I rarely spoke to him until my mother started getting ill. The night after Mother had passed, we were sitting at the dining room table when somehow my sexuality came up in the conversation.

"The Bible tells us that homosexuality is a sin, but

Aunt Jerry and I still love you," my uncle said.

Although I was grateful they had been there for my mother in her last years of life, and for me, too, I did not understand how they could love me without really knowing me. A lot of time had passed since I was the little boy he knew, and a lot of things had happened that changed me. I guess I had always feared they thought the worst of me once everyone in my family found out I was gay after years of hiding the truth. My fears and family dynamics had weakened the bridge between us. The time had come to reinforce it so we could stand in the middle and let the waters of the past, full of estrangement, wash away under our feet.

I made my way to the front door.

"Cold enough for you?" he asked.

"Yes. Very!"

"Well, get yourself in here and get warmed up."

It was good to see him as he welcomed me in and led me through the properly set living room to the kitchen that could have been modeled out of one featured in an issue of *Better Homes & Gardens* magazine. The house smelled like bacon and eggs. My aunt was sitting at the kitchen table, securely bundled up in a colorful housecoat as she attentively tended to a steaming cup of coffee. The house felt as warm as I imagined the coffee. My aunt does not like being cold.

"Can you believe it, Jerry? The boy made it," my uncle joked.

She starts to get up to offer a hug. I motioned to her to stay seated, leaning down instead to hug her.

"Can I get you a cup of coffee and something to eat, Dear?" she asked.

"I'm good for now, thanks," I answer, while pulling out a chair next to her from the table.

"Can you believe it's been just over a year?" Aunt Jerry asked.

My uncle and I gave the same response of "no" at the same time. We looked at each other, smiling a smile of sadness as I sat down.

"Have you talked to your sister?" my aunt questioned.

"No, not since she moved back to Warner Robins last month and was arrested for the third time."

"Well, she is a troubled soul like your mother. Sandra gave your uncle a heart attack while she was living in Fayette!" Aunt Jerry added.

"She got arrested again?" my uncle asked.

"Yes, mostly for drunkenness and disorderly conduct, but I don't want to talk about that now. I want to talk about my mother."

"Okay, Son."

"I'm anxious to go back to the farm and see the high school where you and Mother went."

Our conversation shifted. We talked about the funeral, just passing its year anniversary. Then the weather and how cold it was then and how cold it is now. Everyone was grateful that the temperature was rising. The conversation shifted back to Mother and to their high school.

"The old high school is in walking distance of the house," my uncle informs.

"Does it still look the same?"

"Oh, yes. They added on to it many years ago, but it looks the same from the front. Not much has altered it except for the addition."

"Then we should go there first, don't you think?"

"Good idea. You know your mother just loved

school."

"Yes, I do. Remember she made me go to college. She was relentless about me going even though I resisted. She could be very persuasive, you know."

"That was your mother, alright. School was very important to her. Let's bundle ourselves up and face the cold," my uncle said.

Within minutes, I found myself walking up the same cement sidewalk my mother had happily strolled on the high school campus. I knew it was such an important place for her. It was an escape and a way to get out of Fayette.

"Look at those arches at the top of the stairs," I pointed out.

"Yes, lots of school children have hurried under them over the years. I can almost see your mother standing on the stairs carrying her books. She was a smart one, your mother."

"Yes, she was in many ways."

"She was so proud of you when you started Mercer. The first one from our family to go to college."

"Yeah. I wished she could have been the first instead of me."

"Well, Son. You made her happy by sticking it through and graduating."

"So, I understand you're substitute teaching here," I commented, as he held the door to the entrance open for me.

"Yes. I can only play golf so many days."

"Is it strange being back here, I mean, after having retired from a career and you're walking the halls of where you used to get into trouble?"

"What do you mean into trouble?" my uncle asked.

"Well, I remember Mother telling me a time or two you liked to play pranks on the teachers."

Uncle Ben laughs.

"Well, maybe a few now and then. All harmless."

"So, what was it like? Tell me what mother was like at school."

"She was serious about school, loved everything about it. She loved to read. She read every book she could get her hands on. Your mother always had a book in her hands if she wasn't picking cotton. And all the teachers loved your mother. School and books were her escape from the poor rural life into which she was born."

"I know."

"She was so excited her senior year. Your mother had such big plans after school. I remember her on yearbook day like it was yesterday," my uncle told me.

And I could almost see her in my mind, a young Mary Ellen as she walks down the central hallway of Fayette County High School in her ankle-high white socks and somewhat worn, brown-leather loafers at lunchtime. Her plaid just-below-the-knee skirt playfully fans out with each joyful step. Her arms are crossed over the 1949 thirteenth volume of her senior yearbook, *The Echo*. It is pressed tightly against the pink button-up sweater she is so proud of wearing. She bought it at the year-end basement sale at Hodges Department Store with her first paycheck from Scott's—an old trolley car turned into a burger place, where all the kids hung out after high school, that she worked at a few hours a week when she was not needed on the farm. She had kept all her yearbooks. I sat in my office one afternoon spending several hours going through each one. The coveted book, where everyone passes it around to be autographed with words of admiration, good wishes, and brief reminders of the past year's events. All of which to be re-read decades later, to remember who sat behind her in Mrs. Houston's history class tugging her hair to pass a note over to the blonde boy with the vivid green eyes on the next aisle. Or remember the lanky, but dreamy, dark, wavy-haired boy named Leonard Cannon, from the basketball team, who always asked to copy her algebra homework before class with a subtle, slight stutter, and most likely had a huge crush on her, but too shy to ask her to the Friday night football game or just for a cola after school.

This and more is all concealed between the covers, serving as a time capsule that has become worn and tattered, and lost in a pile of other books of various sizes and subject matter on a bookshelf in the dark hallway of my mother's home. But back then, on that very day, she could feel the tight binding of the book and smell the fresh printed ink on each of the 127 crisp white pages. They have a yellow tint and are brittle now, and the messages in fading ink are not as easily readable. The black-and-white pictures are not as crisp—and have faded, too—as they were on that day when my mother first held the yearbook in her arms and close to her chest. Betty Sue Shelton writes:

You are the "cutest and sweetest girl" and smart, too. I wish you lots of good luck in the future.

Janette Rasberry, in "Favorites" writes:

Mary Ellen, I think you are cute and have very pretty hair. Love always.

The devilishly handsome football star, Rayford Shephard, wrote:

Best wishes to one of the funniest and cutest girls I know. I hope you have a wonderful future!

Her favorite teacher, Mrs. Roy Martin, writes in big scrip:

Dear "Adopted Child," You know what's going on, do you not? I've fallen "lock stock and barrel" for your ruddy cheeks, your dancing eyes and your merry disposition.

"Mrs. Martin had a reputation as a very hard English teacher," my uncle told me. He went on to say she demanded excellence and would not settle for anything less. She required all the students to subscribe to *The Readers Digest*. Each student had to learn the meaning of all the words in the vocabulary section and write papers on various articles. Although widely feared and disliked by many students, Mary Ellen thought the sun rose and set with Mrs. Martin. Her goal was to prepare her students for college and she taught her classes accordingly. One year, she gave all the students Fs, but was later convinced by the principal to give a make-up final. Some students went to summer school before their senior year to avoid her class, while others transferred to Hubbervilles High School, fifteen miles away, for their senior year.

When other kids dreaded each new school day, Mary Ellen was at the edge of the dirt road eagerly waiting for the bus to take her away. Take her away from the cotton fields that she would have to return to in the afternoon.

"Mrs. Martin sensed the void in your mother's spirit and the unhappiness of her home life that she tried to hide under her enthusiasm," my uncle told me. My mother was eager to learn all that Mrs. Martin had to teach her. It is obvious in her yearbook message that she saw promise in this young girl named Mary Ellen and wanted to nurture her. My mother indeed was her adopted daughter. Mrs. Martin had a son, and found a daughter when my mother

97

first walked into her classroom. There, my mother found a world outside of rural Alabama and the difficult home life.

We continued to walk the halls not saying much after that. My uncle introduced me to the principal and a few of the teachers.

"Room 12. That was your mother's homeroom. Mrs. Thomson, I think was the teacher's name."

"Really."

A laugh flew out of my uncle's mouth.

"What's so funny?"

"Ah, I was just remembering how all the boys would follow your mother around the halls between classes."

"So, the boys liked her?"

"Oh yeah. Your granddaddy had to chase a few of them off the farm with his shotgun a time or two."

"Really?"

I looked into the classroom through the little window in center of the door. There was a sixth-grade class in progress listening to the teacher as she talked and wrote on the blackboard.

"Well, you ready to see what's left of the old farm?" my uncle asked.

"Can we come back again sometime to the school?"

"Of course. Anytime you want."

We stopped back by the house to check on Dugan and get the Rover. Still early, the road was quiet and still empty of traffic as my uncle drove. Obviously, he was more familiar with the way back to the farm, about thirty minutes or so from the small town. It was hard to believe so much time had passed and I was back. After my last visit with my mother thirty-three years ago, I had felt there was no reason for me to return. At that time, my grandmother had a stroke and was put in a nursing home. By then, my grandparents had left the farm, too old for the hard labor that had been such a day-to-day existence for them for so long. They moved into a one bedroom apartment in town.

On that trip, my mother and I went directly to the nursing home after arriving into town. At the time I was in my first year at Mercer. We found my grandfather and uncle sitting in the sparse, white room as my grandmother lay childlike in the bed, her eyes open, but with little expression. Uncle Ben asked me to take my grandfather back home. He had been up all night. The apartment was only a few miles away; everything was in close proximity in the small town, but the car ride seemed longer. I could not help but think about the span of years that had passed since I last saw my grandparents during that car ride—I was a child then; now I was a young man in college. Oddly enough, Grandfather had not changed, but I had. Understandably, the conversation was filled with his and my grandmother's ailments. He had lost sight in one eye and had a cataract in the other.

"I'm sorry about Grandmother. How are you holding up?" I asked.

"Good as can be expected, I guess."

He still dressed like a farmer in his Sears' brand of denim overalls with a white shirt underneath, and the old, felt hat he had worn in the fields to keep the sun off his head. He was never without the shiny, silver pocket watch, which I had been mesmerized by as a child and would sit in his lap playing with it like it was a toy. He smelled the same as I had remembered, too. Musty like the old Ford pickup with the dented fenders he used to drive, and like aged cheese and freshly plowed dirt.

99

I was not aware that the apartment was in subsidized housing and that they lived in the projects until he told me to turn off the main road. The buildings were generic: brick, small porches, an occasional broken window, a few wrecked and broken-down cars parked on the streets and residents hanging out in the front of grass-overgrown, weed-infested yards.

My grandfather started talking about the neighbors. I could tell he was embarrassed to be living there and I sensed he wished he was back on the farm. His life now represented how fragile and physically weak he had become—drained by the years of hard, unrelenting toil. Then out of nowhere the "N" word comes out of his mouth referring to a group of young men, of working age, hanging out on the corner in the middle of a weekday. Out of shock, I almost choked on the gasp of air that rushed in my mouth and down into my throat. I forced myself to bite my tongue, realizing it was fruitless to try to educate him at this point in his life. He was old, and his ideals were deeply—extremely—rooted in the Civil War South. I knew at that moment I would never come back to Fayette again. The previous fear of how I felt my mother would react to the fact I was gay, rose up again, and I knew my grandfather would not embrace a gay grandson. So, I never returned, not even for my grandparents' funerals. I regret that decision now that I am reunited with my aunt and uncle.

Uncle Ben slowed down the Rover as we approached a bend in the road. I recognized the abandoned white, wooden building, intimately positioned off to the side on the left. The sign, "Folcome's Grocery," still hung over the door; although severely weathered and faded, it was legible. It was a picture from the past; a smile came to my lips reminding me of the many times I had walked to it with my mother as a child. The proprietor always gave me a piece of hard mint candy to put in my bottle of Coca-Cola for the walk home.

I was apprehensive as the Rover veered off the blacktop onto the gravel and dirt. The sound is distinctive, even with closed eyes—tires rolling over dirt roads.

"Can you pull over for a second?" I asked.

He started to question me, but complied with my request. We both sat quietly.

"Do you come back here very much?" I asked.

"No, not much," he answered.

Timidly, I leaned my body into the windshield in order to look as far down the road as possible, looking beyond the bend that sluggishly curved off to the right for any signs of life. But everything was still under the clean, February late morning sky. I tried to remember, to see in my mind, my mother and I walking over the dirt road. My uncle switched off the ignition key, mentioning something about high gas prices and not wanting to waste any. The hum of the motor stopped, intensifying the silence. I released my seatbelt before peeling off my heavy jacket. I felt a hint of the lack of sleep from the night before, but I was wired from the Diet Cokes. Somehow the caffeine and sleep deprivation have evened each other out. I thought about Dugan for a second, wondering if he was behaving for Aunt Jerry. My mind returns its concentration to what is in front of me. Then, it all comes into focus, like time traveling thousands of miles an hour backwards; the sky lowers as the silhouettes become three dimensional: the road, the shadows crossing it, the treetops, and the quiet that belongs to this place only and no other on earth.

Rushing Road

It is two childhoods and two generations that began under a clear-blue infinite sky, where the sun indolently peeks over a horizon made seemingly of never-ending rows of snowy white cotton and jade corn stalks standing in the early, colorless mist of an Alabama morning. To the east, the corn stands sturdy and lofty in their multitude; row after row making a maze-within-a-maze in the landscape. To the west are fields covered in low prickly cotton plants as far as a little boy's eyes can see. This is what I remember. I was that little boy, and now he is looking through the eyes of a grown man. The fields are empty today, not having been farmed in many years. This was the land worked by my Grandfather Rushing; small in comparison to those of the larger farms that once stamped the vast landscape. When he farmed it, he walked every inch be-

103

hind a plow pulled by a mule. There is still some hint of the straight, even furrows, but most of the fields have been reclaimed by the wilderness from which they were originally carved.

In the myriad there stood a lone, weather-beaten wooden, tin-roofed, four-room rickety farmhouse resting on irregularly shaped stacked stones. Six wide creeping steps—all with an irregular rise—led up to a long front porch, where a swing hung motionless in the still air. To a little boy, the wooden steps seemed big and arduous, almost not scaleable without the assistance of a loving mother's hand to keep balance while conquering each one at a time.

The house sat several yards back from a dirt road, its front yard void of grass. Two parallel flower beds, outlined with softball-size rocks, usher family and visitors alike up the well-traveled path leading to the front steps. Across from the house was an old, tilting barn held up by a mighty tree that had grown into its side. It was the home of the plow-mule, Old Blue, who had a talent for opening the latch of the wooden gate with his mouth.

A garden, with a variety of vegetables, including squash, and an assortment of berries and melons, grew alongside the south side of the house, separating it from the fields of snow and jade. Devotedly, it produced big red strawberries covering all of the little boy's hand, as he vigilantly plucked each one and dropped them in his grandmother's fetching basket; his mind tasting the sweet, delicious pies to come.

A stone-constructed well, just steps from the back porch, was dug deep into the ground, calling farm workers to quench their thirst with its pure, ice cold water. A tin bucket hanging on a rope often dripped water from a recent draw.

Most of this will probably be gone now. My uncle knows this is an emotional moment for me. He continues to sit quietly in the driver's seat. I think how patient he is, and how he was at times with my mother.

"Let's go see," I tell him.

He starts up the engine. The Rover's large, broad tires heavily crunch over the gravel and dirt as my uncle slowly turns it up the road. I hit the down arrow on the switch for the electric window. The smell of country rushes in. It is clean and fresh, and old at the same time.

"How far is it up the road?" I ask.

"Just a few miles."

"That's what I remember."

It is surreal being back, traveling this way again, listening to the crackle and pop of the road; looking out the open window at the trees, and the fields—now empty.

"There it is," my uncle announces.

"I know. I can tell."

He pulls the Rover off to the side where the barn once stood. I think about Old Blue and feeding him with my grandfather. Part of the wooden and barbwire fencing once installed to keep him from roaming off remains intact along the road. I remember pushing ears of corn through the chucker in the barn as if it was a childhood toy and feeding the kernels to the chickens.

I look across the road to see that most of the farmhouse is gone, too. We cross over to it, and I hear and feel the dirt and gravel under my shoes, triggering recollections in my mind. The sound of the crunching and sensation of the gravel is the same as I remember from when I walked here as a little boy. Funny, I think, it does not seem that long ago. Not that long ago at all. My uncle tells me that some of the wood the house was made of was re-used to mend other houses and barns in the area. What could not be salvaged was left to continue to deteriorate and become a part of the earth again. Only the stones it rested on remain, as does the lower section of the fire-place. A few yards over, the tin, A-framed roof of the old well has collapsed partly on top of its opening. I peer down into the hole in the earth. Inquisitively I pick up a small rock from the ground by my feet and drop it into the cavernous hole to see if there is still water down there. The sound of a subtle splash satisfies my curiosity.

I turn around to walk the rooms of the house or, rather, where they used to be. I start in the front, where the six wide steps once supported many feet up and down. Then, over the porch, where I had sat in the swing with my mother on many occasions, that made a melancholy whine every time she powered it with a swift kick of her heel off the weathered, wooden floor as we waited for a car or truck to drive by, watching the dust fly up as we waved to its occupants. We then continued swinging back and forth, back and forth while listening to the quiet and watching the corn and cotton grow. I can almost hear the screen door slam behind me as I walk over the area that was once the living room and stand in front of the fireplace that warmed us on many chilly nights. The smell of burning wood, hissing and crackling sounds it made comes back to me.

This room was also where my grandparents slept in an iron-framed bed positioned across from the fireplace, against the wall that separated it from the kitchen. I take the few steps to where my mother's old room was, where she spent her childhood reading and dreaming, singing and playing, laughing and crying. Where, as a young woman, she returned with me in her belly. I stand where her bed was, where she held me as a little boy for afternoon naps. I walk into the kitchen where the old, wood-burning stove heated up cold mornings, while baking biscuits for breakfast and cornbread for supper. A dozen steps to the right, I am in my great-grandmother's and uncle's room. I step to the back porch where I took baths in a round metal tub filled with well water heated from the stove. All the children shared the same bath water; the lesser of the dirtier ones went first. I walk down the back steps and across the yard to where the outhouse once stood, before it deteriorated into a few scattered pieces of termite-eaten wood. I remembered hating to use it, dreadfully afraid a snake or spider, or a nasty splinter was just waiting for me to sit on the wooden shelf with the round hole cut out of it.

I know my uncle is moved as well, seeing me here again.

"Uncle Ben," I call out.

He is leaning against the mature, black walnut tree that stands to the left of one of the cotton fields, its branches reaching out and up into the sky like long, thick aged arms and fingers. The tree is as big as I remembered it when I would climb up on its bulky roots that travel deep into the ground anchoring it to the earth, and sat eating a handful of cookies or homemade ice cream dripping down the cone making my hands sticky and sweet. God, I think. What this tree must know and all the things that its long reaching limbs have shaded throughout the years. Like a guardian, it is still strong, overseeing the land that now sits idle.

"How old do you think that tree is?" I ask.

My uncle looks up in my direction.

"Goodness, at least over a hundred. Give or take a few years. It was a mature tree when your mother and I were children."

"Hey. Do you remember when I was just a little boy and you chased me around the house with a fish you had just caught in the pond down below the old barn?"

"I don't recall," he answers.

"Well, it was so long ago, but I've always remembered that day like it was yesterday. You really pissed me off."

And, then I remember what a devilishly handsome man my uncle was, but I do not tell him.

My uncle laughed and I see that lady-killer smile of his spread from ear to ear, showing off his deep dimples.

This is my home, I tell myself. This is where it all began for me and for my mother. I am compelled to reach down and touch the earth, to dig with my fingernails and scoop up the dirt in my hands. I examine and feel the soil I had excavated that so much had grown from, not only crops but the births of those before me and even my mother. I look back over the fields, the dirt still in my hands, and think about the life my mother lived on this very plot of land, and the history made under the vast Alabama sky over my head.

Many years ago, it was a land cultivated by hardships and long days of sweat-producing labor. Wealthy landowners created large cotton plantations which greatly depended on slavery. Slaves by the thousands were forced to work the fields. Thus began Alabama's rich history of cotton production in the 1830's. With the huge demands for the product, the state crop became known as "King Cotton." At its peak, it made many landowners rich, from the misery and heartache of the slaves, and sparked an enormous migration—in the beginning—referred to as "Alabama Fever" from neighboring states, as well as, other areas of the country.

After slavery was abolished in 1865, many "ex" slaves continued to work the fields for very little compensation. Then, in 1910, with the Great Migration, large numbers of African Americans moved to the Northern and Midwestern industrial areas for better opportunities than in the South where they were still often treated like slaves. Alabama suffered great economic losses and began to move into an agricultural depression, which eventually left it a very poor state. With the state still tied to cotton, many poor whites began to tend the fields. Men with no or very little money from other vocations became sharecroppers in hopes of making a better life for themselves and their families. Typically, they were provided a house, fertilizer, seed and a mule to plow a certain number of acres. It was hard; involved sun-up to sundown work, plowing the fields, and then later, back-breaking picking of the cotton by hand. For all their work, they received only a small share of the profits, resulting in a minimal existence where very few were able to improve their situation. As their predecessors, the sharecroppers became slaves to the cotton and it became the Master.

My grandfather was one of those sharecroppers. His father died when he was nine years old. In his early life, he worked in the coal mines until they were picked dry. Without much of an education, all he had was a strong back to make a living. He then became a farmer. He worked one-hundred acres owned by Mr. Gardner, who was a second father to him. My grandfather's father's sister had married Mr. Gardner's son. I remember my grandfather as extraordinarily tall and lanky. His shoulders, wide and stiff, like a tree trunk was under his shirt. His skin was a dark coffee color from laboring long days under the sun. Deeply embedded lines and crisscrossing wrinkles covered his face from his forehead to his Adam's apple. His eyes were dark brown and deeply set in their sockets, surrounded by broad, long-reaching crow's feet from their corners to his ears. His cheek bones were spherical and the size of golf balls, and his lips, thin and wide curving downward to his chin. To a little boy, his oversized, sandpaper hands seemed monstrous. When he spoke, his voice struggled from his vocal cords, making cavernous, husky words leave his mouth.

He married Farris Berry, the daughter of a farmer. She was tall, too, and willowy, with a sweet face and stood straight as a board. My grandmother's family did not approve of the marriage, believing my grandfather, being a sharecropper, was beneath her status. After the marriage, she moved into the small farmhouse with her new husband and mother-in-law; close quarters to say the least. A four-room house was not large enough for two strong, willful women and they often battled and bickered for control—mixing about as well as oil and water. During the years following the marriage, their relationship proved to be a volatile one. It was clear that my Great-Grandmother Rushing, deceivingly appearing to be a petite whisper of a woman, with years of hard labor etched on her face and a backbone of steel, was the matriarch. She had lived a hard life raising four children practically alone after her husband had suddenly died. My grandmother did not always agree with her mother-in-law's decisions. They were like two lionesses fighting for control over their pride. But they acted much differently from the lionesses in the wild that are the hunters for their group and capture their prey with precise and complex teamwork.

The house was drafty in winter. The cold winds rushed through the cracks, weakly kept at bay by the single fireplace in the front room and the wood-burning stove in the kitchen. At night, feather beds and layers of handmade quilts kept the chilly air off well-clothed, layered bodies. It was the reverse in summer, with the escalating southern heat roasting every corner of the house. The only air conditioning was an occasional tepid breeze moving thickly through open windows.

It was a hard existence, especially for a young girl named Mary Ellen, who yearned to be somewhere else and live someone else's life. For an outsider, it made for an idealistic picture of a rural, simple life in a small northern Alabama farm community. Norman Rockwell images come to mind of a scene from the kitchen, a great-grandmother sitting at the table eating biscuits covered in skillet gravy, as the roosters outside the window called another sunrise. The wood-fueled stove crackled as the smells of sausage and eggs filled the awakening house. A farmer and his wife working side-by-side to bring in the crops, as their two young children helped as much as their little bodies allowed. But, that was not the case. It was not the true picture of my mother's childhood and could never show the real struggles and hardships as well as the tragedies covered up by the painter's brush.

Farmers did not work by the clock, but rather by the sun. A daily labor began before the sun showed its first ray of light, graying over the cotton. By then, the family had already eaten their breakfast and was in the fields. The work day ended after the sun withdrew from the sky. The main reason for an early start was to try to get the bulk of the work done before the day grew too hot. Everyone worked in the fields, including the children, as soon as they were old enough to help in caring for the crops. Mary Ellen worked right along with her father, mother, grandmother and brother before and after school. During the harvest, she would have to put her education on hold to help, sometimes for several weeks. Her main job was to hoe the cotton. Almost as early as she was able to play with her rag-doll, she learned how to "chop the cotton." In order to insure a large yield, cotton was planted with an excessive amount of seeds. If left alone, the fields would become over-crowded. They had to be thinned by cutting out some of the plants with a hoe. This action was called "chopping cotton" due to the action of hacking out sections of plants since proper spacing was about the width of a hoe. The fields had to be kept clear of grass and weeds as well. Her father wanted every sprig of grass removed and would make her do it over if she missed a single blade. A proud man, he wanted his fields to be the best looking, with the straightest rows in the county.

My Grandfather Rushing had a love/hate relationship with the land and with the crops it birthed. The land was wild, and had to be constantly tended to keep it tame. But there was only so much he could do or require of his family to make the cotton grow. The fields were at the mercy of the weather, and insects were a constant enemy. The climate conditions were especially important because the crops needed the right amount of rain while the young plants were coming up and beginning to grow. Too little rain would inhibit the growth, while too much would wash them away. In the fall, when the cotton is opening, less rain is better to insure that the white balls will pop out nice and fluffy. Too much rain makes the fibers wet and soggy, resulting in rot in extreme cases. For the farm families, the days ended in fatigue. It was a consumed life of worry over the weather, the crops and the pending harvest.

When the cotton did not need attention, there were other chores around the house for everyone. Mary Ellen helped out in the kitchen and cleaning of the house. She tended to the feeding of the chickens and gathering the eggs, while daydreaming of a different life far away from the hard work of farm life.

Each working day, about mid-morning, her mother and grandmother would head back to the house to prepare lunch, which was called dinner. The evening meal was referred to as supper. Almost everything needed for food was produced on the farm. The cow supplied plenty of milk, which was kept in jugs, tied to sticks and submerged in the spring to keep it cold during the spring and summer months, or during unusually warm stretches. The chickens supplied the eggs; whereas the garden offered lots of vegetables and berries. In good years, there was even enough to give to the surrounding neighbors or sell in town. Meat consisted of an occasional chicken. From time to time, one would be selected and placed in a pin by itself where, for a few weeks, it would be fed extra corn to fatten it up. Then, Great-Grandmother Rushing would take the plumped chicken to the chopping block. The feathers were collected and saved for pillow or mattress stuffing.

Another form of meat was salt-cured pork, usually referred to as "fat back." Since there was no refrigeration, hogs were not killed until the weather turned cold enough to keep the meat from spoiling. Supper on hog killing day was a special event. The meal consisted of hot biscuits, fresh pork tenderloin and gravy. The ham part of the hog was smoked or salt-cured. A large portion of the lean parts were ground for sausages, cooked and then canned in jars that would keep through the winter months. The fatty parts of the hog were cooked down to make lard. Other fatty parts were used to make soap. Corn from the field was taken to the grist mill to be ground into meal for cornbread, a major staple at most of the daily meals. One of the few things that needed to be purchased was flour. It came in large cloth sacks. Once the sacks were emptied, Mary Ellen's grandmother would make garments like shirts and blouses from the cloth of both the flour and seed sacks. Mary Ellen never liked to wear the homemade sack clothes, but did when she had no other option. Nothing was discarded on the farm; everything was repurposed if possible.

When she could stand on her shadow, it meant the sun was overhead and time to head to the house for dinner. After eating, everyone would find the coolest place possible to rest before returning to the heat of the fields for many more long hours of work. Finally, when the sun began to set on top of the cotton to the west, Mary Ellen knew the daylight would soon be leaving the sky and she could find a reprieve until the next day.

I took one last look back over the fields surrounding the spot where the house once stood, standing on its decay. I imagined my grandfather's silhouette plowing the fields under a spring sky, season after season, getting them ready for the seeds. Then in June, walking down the rows as the plants began to bud with white flowers greeting the early morning. I could almost see him wiping his forehead, as the summer days grew long, as he watched the flowers turn pink, and later purple; eventually shedding, as small bolls appeared; and waiting for August, praying the conditions would stay right so the round balls of white would blanket the fields.

As I turned to walk back to the road, I noticed the absence of the peach trees, which once grew up on the hill behind the outhouse. At that moment, I could almost taste their sweetness and feel the juice running down my chin after taking the first bite into their furry flesh. The sassafras trees are gone, too.

"We should be heading on back. Your aunt is making dinner."

"You mean lunch?"

"No. Remember, around here lunch is called dinner," my uncle corrects.

We cross the road back to the Rover. The sound of walking on dirt and gravel fills the air again. My mind instantly wanders back. Suddenly, I feel my mother's presence and know she has met me back here and is walking next to me, and my uncle, too. Walking back up the road singing a song she has stuck in her head.

As the Rover pulls away, I look back at the footprint of the house. In my mind, I see my mother holding my hand, guiding me up the wide wooden steps. She lifts me onto the porch swing and takes a seat next to me. It squeaks as she pushes us off with a kick of her foot.

"Do you see the road sign?" my uncle asks, as he stops the Rover at the end of the dirt road.

I do not hear him, distracted by my reminiscing.

"Randy?"

"Yes. What did you say?"

"Do you see the road sign out your window, Son?"

I turn my head to look out. The car is idling right next

to it.

"Rushing Road," I read out loud.

"What's that all about?" I asked my uncle.

"A few years back, the county renamed the numbered roads, and since us Rushings lived and farmed this land for so long, it was named Rushing Road. After your grandfather."

"Wow, did Mother know that?"

"I'm not sure. I think that was done after the last high school reunion she came to. Not sure if I ever thought to mention it to her," he said, as he cleared his throat.

I can sense my uncle is thinking about her as he sighs. His eyes turn misty and his face sad.

"What happened to her?" I asked.

"To who?"

"To Mother. What do you think really happened to her? I mean, why did everything fall apart for her?"

"You know about as much as I do. Life is not fair to everyone. Your mother had a lot of struggles; we both did growing up. It was brutal at times on the farm."

"I know."

"But, I will tell you this, she did change. She left the farm with so much optimism. I guess I should have forced her to come back with me to Fayette when you guys were little."

"I remember."

"Yeah. I regret she didn't leave your father then."

"That was right after he tried to divorce Mother, but I told him I would not leave her. He wanted to take us kids and just leave her after all he had taken from her. After he had hurt her so deeply."

"She ended up a lot like your grandmother, our mother," Uncle Ben said.

He went on to tell me that their mother suffered from periods of depression and frequent mood swings. At sixteen, while standing on the back porch of her father's farmhouse drinking water during a thunderstorm, she was struck by lighting. She had commented that it felt like she was drinking fire. Not long after that, her personality changed. One minute she could be nice and the next, mean as the devil. This behavior continued into adulthood.

"Mary Ellen and I knew when the change was coming."

He continued to tell me that they called the change "the other self." I learned that their mother would have a bizarre, vacant gaze in her eyes. She would stay up all night drinking black coffee at the kitchen table. The next day she would be vicious, cursing and screaming at the top of her lungs, lashing out at her mother-in-law. Once she threw her husband's mother's clothes in the yard and told her to leave. There were other outbursts during these mood swings where she once pushed her mother-in-law off the porch and another when she hit her repeatedly with a broom. Uncle Ben went on to tell me that their grandmother was very feisty herself. Sometimes the fights between his mother and grandmother got so physical and out of control that his father would have to step in. Uncle Ben told me his father always took up for his mother.

"There were times when Daddy chased our mother into the corn fields, waving his 22 rifle threatening to shoot her. I would run under the house or head to the woods to hide in a foxhole I had dug to play war games. I would sit and wait for the gunshot. Mary Ellen would intercede, running into the fields to try to stop them, standing between her mother and the gun. This went on for years," Uncle Ben told me with sadness in his telling.

117

"I never knew that."

"Well, Daddy never shot Mother, thank God. But she had black eyes and bruises from both our father and Grandmother," my uncle stated.

The violence she witnessed as a young girl followed Mary Ellen into her adulthood. As her parents aged, their personal strife diminished, but the cycle continued in my mother's adult years.

I turn my head around and looked out the rear window of the Rover. I had come home again. I had come back to Rushing Road and to the land that was unable to totally break her spirit.

Cries in the Night

Most families have their secrets; skeletons hurriedly hidden away in deep, dark places in hopes of never being discovered. But, no matter how bottomless their resting place, they are never deep enough to be forgotten by the guardians who carry the burden of the truth and the knowledge that the event occurred.

For the longest time, I was not aware of all the ghosts haunting my mother other than that of my father. Although I know he played a large role in her inability to pull herself out of the pool of mental agony she was submerged in and stay out from under the cloud of depression that overcast many years of her life, there was another ghost I only heard her talk to a few times. Usually, late at night, as she had my father's.

"Why did you do that? Why? Why? Why did you do that?" she would say to herself.

Commonly, my mother would stay up late, sometimes never going to bed for several days. She was consumed with a restlessness that would not allow her to sleep peacefully. When she did go to bed, she would lie down with her eyes wide opened looking at the ceiling. Constantly, she rubbed her feet together—sole over heel—for hours. If within earshot of her room, I could hear the sound of the resulting friction generated by the action leaving the tops of her feet red and chafed. One of her arms would be positioned at her side with the other rested across her forehead, while her fourth fingers made a circular movement around the thumbs of each hand. More often she rambled throughout the rooms of the small house—from her bedroom to the kitchen to the breakfast room—into the sluggish hours of the morning, still making the circular movement with her fingers and thumbs as she walked. Occasionally, I would hear the idiosyncratic whine of the living room door open and then close, within seconds, as if she were looking for something or someone. Finally, she would settle down for a brief period, sitting at the kitchen table drinking, sometimes just coffee, as she continued the ritual with her feet and fingers.

I would lie in bed in deep concern for her as the low volume of the music she loved to listen to, and the smoke from her lit cigarettes, crept through the house. She took in long inhales, followed by low, extended sighs exhaling a bit of the anguish that was constantly fermenting inside her. On the nights she was drinking alcohol, I would hear the popping of beer cans, or the clanging of the liquor bottle, hitting the rim of her glass as she refilled it again and again, trying to silence the ghosts in her head by drowning herself in liquor.

She often talked in a low whisper as if engaged in conversation with someone sitting across the table from her. Many times her words were garbled, but filled with emotion. Other times they were clear, but their meaning ambiguous as if she was playing some kind of word game or spouting off some childhood nursery rhyme.

"Mommy, the baby's crying. Can't you hear the baby? He's hungry. Mommy, feed the baby."

Over and over she recited the rhyme until the night was eradicated by the approaching daylight, but the darkness lingered in her soul, as the ghost of her little brother returned to haunt her. This is what I know.

My mother was nine-years-old, old enough to remember. Uncle Ben was four. Most of the bulk of the crop had been harvested. On that final day—that led into night— the only cotton present were discolored and diminutive balls widely scattered randomly in the well-picked field under the black and white sky. The pre-night air was still thick as the day's, and oddly, unseasonably filled with heat. As the sky darkened, the stars in the heavens appeared further away than usual; their light struggling to infiltrate what seemed like a sheet of syrupy haze. A half dollar-sized moon appeared, offering just enough light to guide Mary Ellen as she wearily walked down the path that led to the house. She let out a sigh of relief, feeling unfettered after having unhappily missed almost two weeks of school to help pick the remaining cotton.

Every morning, from the field, she heard the roar of the school bus' engine as it made its way over the dirt road. Mary Ellen stopped her picking, regrettably watching it pass her by, filling the air with a solid mass of throat choking dust, until it settled back on the ground as the bus was long on its way. And each morning, Mary Ellen wanted to discard her sack of cotton strapped across her back and hanging off the side of her hip—already a quarter filled by the time the bus passed—and run after it. For every one ball picked, it seemed there were millions more to gather—one at a time—until her bag weighed as much as she did.

As the day had progressed, the crows took wing overhead screaming their calls to a relentless sun growing larger and larger, hotter and hotter. By noon, she was drenched in sweat. Mary Ellen could feel the heat of the past weeks on her skin even though she had worn a straw hat. The back of her neck was red and burned from the unforgiving sun stretching over the fields and on everyone and everything that ventured out of the shade. Her glove-covered hands hurt from the frequent pricks of the thorns from which they were worn to protect. As did her arms, tender and swollen, covered in ripped, blood-stained long sleeves of her flour-sack shirt that held in the heat. Her young back ached from the constant bending over.

Several times during the picking, she stopped to look over the field—as far past it as her height and eyes would allow—toward the dirt road that she knew would one day lead her away; to the day she would never have to pick cotton again. Tomorrow, she could go back to school.

She looked over her shoulder, calling out to her brother to follow. He was lagging behind, carrying an oil-burning lantern giving off a feeble glow. Really too young to pick much cotton, he had stuck by her side a good part of the day. It was Mary Ellen's job to keep an eye on him. So, he would follow her through the rows of cotton picking ten balls to her one hundred. Not far behind him was their father, scarcely visible in the darkening landscape, looking back over the field, as he took a final survey to be sure every usable ball of cotton had been collected. He had been under a lot of pressure to get the crop in on time before the rains encroached as predicted by the trusted Farmer's Almanac. There was a science to knowing when to pick the cotton, something Mary Ellen's father had learned by trial and error, heartache and triumph, year after year. The cotton had to be collected within ten days after the leaf drop to avoid lint discoloration resulting from re-growth and weathering. This had to coincide with having a week or more of low to moderate humidity, high heat and a good, strong unvarying sun in the sky. But it was more like a guessing game, one he had to win in order to provide for his family.

His wife had been unable to spend the long hours needed in the fields due to her pregnancy. The last couple of months had been hard on Mary Ellen's mother, only able to work in the fields until the middle of the seventh month. But she was not one to sit around and wait. There was always something needing attention on the small dirt farm. It was just a matter of days, or even hours, before their third child would enter the world. And, because of the pending birth, Mary Ellen had to take on more responsibilities to help her mother and the family survive.

After a much-appreciated dinner of cornbread, canned tomatoes, green beans and hash, Mary Ellen escapes to her room in the front of the farmhouse. She walks barefoot over the long-planked, squeaking pine floor to her simple, iron-framed bed with its mattress stuffed with chicken feathers. She lights the oil lantern on the small wooden table next to it. Within seconds, a warm glow swells up in the intimate area. She walks to the other side of the room to the wash-table and pours water from the pitcher into a bowl to clean up before changing into a graying night-dress made from another flour sack. With a full belly and refreshed, Mary Ellen returns to her bed. She reaches for the book which she had been reading herself to sleep by the past many nights after laborious days in the field: Dorothea Flothow's, *The Lion and the Unicorn*. She pushes the farm out of her thoughts, allowing the words in the book to send her to a faraway place in her mind.

The evening stretches on, and the oil in the lamp re-cedes as the smell of rain trickles into the room filling Mary Ellen's nostrils. She looks up from the page as a dis-tant clap of thunder, announcing its approach, rumbles through the sky. Then everything goes quiet. She picks up where she had left off on the page. Two more paragraphs into the book, her eyelids begin to feel weighty as sleep draws near. Mary Ellen resists, struggling to keep on read-ing until her eyes finally close. The book and all its char-acters rest on her stomach as she falls into dreams only little girls know.

As the night approaches dawn, the downpour comes as the Almanac had calculated. The dry air engorges the wel-comed moisture leaching through the open windows of the parched house. Another, more deafening clap of thunder explodes in the vicinity within a mile, and a flash of light-ning to the west of the deserted cotton fields electrifies a sinister sky. Mary Ellen jumps up in her bed. The book falls to the floor as the light from the flash banishes the darkness out of the room for a blink of an eye. Then, every thing is gray and shadowy-black again except for the diminutive light of the lantern.

A solid sheet of water encases the house, floods the

fields, and turns the dirt road into a river of mud. Every sound in the house and surrounding farm is drowned out by the onslaught of total wetness. The roar of the rain is constant until the deluge lessens and the sound of water-drops in metal from the leaking roof, dripping into scattered pails and cooking pots on the floor can be heard. What is left of the night quickly turns cold as the wetness eradicates the accumulative heat of many long days and nights. Mary Ellen gets out of bed to close the window. Her bare feet step into a puddle of rainwater on the floor just inside the window. At first it resists her tugs. Once closed, she squashes her face against the glass covered in droplets of rain as the night tenderly cries. The black glass is cool, refreshing her sun-blistered skin. Mary Ellen closes her eyes, takes in a deep breath, and smells the washed air through its thinness.

Now wide awake, she overhears Grandmother Rushing and her father talking in the front room. The coffee brewing on the wood-burning stove flavors the air. She knows something is wrong by the hushed tones in their voices and her mother's muted, whimpers seeping through the thin wall separating the rooms. She suspects the baby is coming.

Mary Ellen slowly opens the door part-way, stopping it just before it can make the creaking noise. She stands— heel over ankle—as the dim light of the small glow from the fireplace seeping into her room highlights her sweet face. She sees her grandmother and father standing amongst the pots and pans filled with rain water under the single light bulb hanging from a black electrical wire in the center of the room. It is the only electricity in the house, installed a year ago. In the shadows, her mother is lying on the bed in the corner. Her belly looks large and swollen as if it is ready to pop under a faded and tattered patchwork quilt. She is holding a damp rag to her forehead. Mary Ellen can tell by her mother's continued low cries and the discomfort on her face that she is in great pain.

"The child is coming soon," her grandmother tells her son.

Mary Ellen is scared. She knows about birth from the animals living on the farm, as well as Sadie's litter of puppies last spring, but the pain on her mother's face is horrifying. Mary Ellen bites her lip.

"Go quickly. Get Haddy Walker and her sister," the matriarch instructs her son.

He grabs his hat from the bench by the door. Mary Ellen runs back to the window in her room. She hears her father push the front door open, then the whine of the screen door. Within seconds, they both slam shut, one after the other. His foot steps are thunderous and heavy on the front porch and down the stairs. She watches her father through the window as he quickly steps out into the wet pre-morning, crossing the muddy dirt road, leaving profound boot prints to the barn. A pallid fog covers the fields. The morning is rapidly approaching as is the baby.

The old Ford truck's engine coughs up, startling the chickens in the adjoining coop. They make a racket as several big, black-gray irregular puffs of smoke spit out of the tailpipe. The wheels spin as they hit the road and large globs of mud take to the air spattering the surface of the truck. Mary Ellen continues to watch until the truck disappears around the bend and into the fog. She returns to the doorway.

"Come here, Child!" her grandmother calls out, after seeing her head peeking out. "Your mother needs you."

Mary Ellen scampers across the floor to her mother's bed.

"Wash out the rag and comfort your mother, Child."

Mary Ellen notices the bed between her mother's legs is wet and mucousy, pinkish-red in color.

"Child, did you hear me?"

She does as her grandmother orders. Her mother bawls out a cry of distress and squeezes her daughter's hand. Hard. Mary Ellen does not speak but her face crunches up with pain. Grandmother Rushing pulls up her daughter-in-law's nightdress and removes the undergarment from her body. It is time to set aside personal rivalries. At least for the time being. A child is on its way.

"Go fetch a pail of water from the well, Child. Hurry!"

Mary Ellen runs out the door of the kitchen and down the stairs of the back porch into the fragile morning. Her bare feet slip on the muddy ground but she does not fall. She stands on the stool by the well, stretching her torso so she can reach in far enough to flip open the wooden cover. Hastily she pulls the rope holding the bucket downward. The crank handle goes around and around in circles until she hears the bucket splash into the water. With both hands she labors at retrieving it back to the top. It is heavy. The full bucket swings back and forth, back and forth as some water spills out, splashing to the bottom of the well. Mary Ellen's hands are still tender from picking the cotton, and even more so from the fibers of the rope irritating them.

Grandmother Rushing meets her on the back porch and takes the pail.

"Go back to your mother, Child," she instructs.

Her grandmother carries the water to the kitchen and pours it into a large kettle sitting on top of the stove. The emptied bucket clangs on the floor as she discards it before leaning down to open the fire door. Quickly she proceeds, sticking more wood inside to accelerate the low flames already burning. A few sparks fly out hitting her in the face, but she is not fazed by their stings.

Mary Ellen has returned to her mother's bedside. She can not look her in the eyes. It is too painful to see her mother like this. She vaguely remembers the birth of her little brother. Suddenly, the roar of her father's pick-up truck announces his return. The noisy engine dies in front of the house. One truck door slams closed, followed by the other. Seconds later, the heavy pounds of her father's boots coming up the steps and across the porch shake the house on its stones. Lighter, hastened, scurrying steps from the two women follow. Their hurried voices enter the house before them. The door flies open as Mary Ellen's father enters with the sisters on his heels. They live several miles up the road on another small farm. They are midwives.

Mary Ellen's mother's labor intensifies. She is balled up on the bed, biting into a pillow as her hands hold her belly.

"Is the water boiling?" asks Haddy, the older and taller of the two sisters.

"It should be close," Grandmother Rushing answers.

Anne, the other sister, shorter and heavier, rushes into the kitchen to check its progress. They have done this many times before. Their mother and grandmother were midwives, too. Within three generations, they have helped bring hundreds of babies into the world.

Ben's sleep is disturbed by all the turmoil. He is standing in the kitchen doorway crying.

"Son, take the boy. This is woman's work now,"

Grandmother Rushing says.

He takes Ben out to the chicken coop to start the daily chores as the sun is filtering through the fog-encroached fields.

Grandmother Rushing instructs Mary Ellen to get more fresh water to wipe the sweat from her mother's face as Anne returns with hot steaming towels in a large pan. Her sister is positioning the mother-to-be on the bed sideways—away from the iron foot of the bed—so she can easily catch the baby when it comes.

"It's going to be okay, Mrs. Rushing," she says, to try to calm her persistent, muted cries. "It will be over soon enough."

Mary Ellen rinses out the rag in the bowl on the table by the bed. She pats it across her mother's face and forehead. The room smells like perspiration. Everyone is sweating, including Mary Ellen.

By now, the morning light has crossed the fields like a crouching animal as it stretches its way through the windows of the house. It is a hopeful light announcing the new day and a new life on its way. Grandmother Rushing takes a seat across the room. Exhaustion from the long night has caught up with her. She will let the midwives do their work.

"The baby is coming!" Haddy calmly calls out moments later.

Grandmother Rushing remains seated. Mary Ellen is shaking as she continues to wipe her mother's face with the rag.

Anne places a warm towel on the bed between Mrs. Rushing legs. The top of the baby's head is sticking out.

"Push. Come on. Push, Honey," Haddy encourages.

Mary Ellen's mother gives out a deep wail.

"That's it, push harder."

Another deep wail leaves her mouth.

"Hold your mother's hand, Sweetie," Anne tells Mary Ellen.

The little girl holds back the tears of fear forming in the corner of her eyes. She wants to run out of the room, but stays put, continuing to do as told. Her mother's grip is strong as she squeezes her hand hard for the second time. Mary Ellen's face crunches again from the pain, but, as before, she does not complain. She can see the back of the baby's head, full of brown, curly, slimy hair. There is blood oozing from her mother's womb staining the towel. Mary Ellen feels sick and wants to run out of the room again, but resists the temptation a second time, keeping her fear at bay as much as a little girl can.

Her mother's cries are continuous as they swell louder. Mary Ellen's father and brother can hear them cross the dirt road as the morning air carries them in all directions. They continue the farm duties. Ben collects the eggs into a basket as his father fills up a long, narrow metal container with chicken feed. One of his mother's extreme cries startles the little boy; the egg in his hand falls to the ground, breaking open at his feet.

"Is Mommy alright?" Ben asks.

"She'll be fine, Son. Finish getting the eggs and don't break any more."

Ben collects another one.

The baby is almost out. Haddy has it partly in the towel.

"Push one more time for me. It's almost over."

Drained, Mrs. Rushing gives all she has in one last push. Her voice is raucous from the hours of moaning and crying.

"It's a boy! You have a son!" Haddy calls out as she pulls the baby the rest of the way. The placenta follows, resting between Mrs. Rushing's legs.

The baby doesn't cry. Anne turns the baby around and begins wiping the thick syrupy-like slime from its face. Then, she looks at Haddy with concern.

"Let me hold my baby," Mrs. Rushing calls out.

"One second, Dear. You just lay still and rest," Haddy responds.

She motions to Anne to address the umbilical cord, which she does by taking a short length of yarn to tie it off before cutting it with a knife she had earlier sterilized in the boiling water.

She then turns to Grandmother Rushing and nods her head to come to the birthing bed. The three women look at the baby, and then at its mother. Mary Ellen rinses out the rag in the bowl of water and wipes her mother's face again. Grandmother Rushing tilts her head down and shakes it in disbelief. Haddy swiftly carries the baby into the kitchen. Her sister and Grandmother Rushing follow.

"Where you going with my baby?" Mrs. Rushing asks.

There is silence for a moment before Anne looks back to answer.

"Just going to clean him up."

Haddy lays the baby on the table in the kitchen. They have only seen this one time before, a child born with such a deformity. The lip of the baby is split, showing a wide gap in the top and a large hole in the roof of its mouth. A cleft-palate-and-lip baby.

"I should go get my son," Grandmother Rushing says with no emotion on her face. She exits the back door.

The midwives began to clean the baby. They talk softly between themselves. Anne shakes her head in concern, for the baby and the mother.

"Tell them to bring my baby," Mrs. Rushing commands her daughter. "I want to hold my baby."

Nursery Rhymes

The day is somber. The cotton fields are picked clean as far as the crows' eyes can see as their wings flitter in the outer realms of the heavens. High over the land they soar, calling out to all who can hear their cries as the fields below sleep. The heat of the extensive days has become an exodus memory as summer dies and the season of Fall seizes its hold, filling the air with smells of tranquil days and crisp nights. The leaves of the trees surrounding the farmhouse are losing their firm hold on the limbs as the westerly winds carry them down to the ground, scurrying them around and around and around. Normally it would be a time to relax and celebrate the birth of an infant boy, but it is anything but that.

A simple, wooden crib sits across the room near the front window. Mary Ellen's father had gotten the crib from the loft of the barn where it had been stored for the past few years along with the rotating hay and sacks of cotton seed.

It was my grandfather's, as well as his siblings' when they were babies, built by their father. After them, it became my mother's, and, after her, Ben's. Now, it is Paul Dean's—the last baby to use it. Many babies had been recited nursery rhymes and sung lullabies while falling asleep in the cherished family crib. Its little feather mattress is covered with a quilt that my grandfather's grandmother had made scores of years ago that has swaddled many newborns. A brown, furry, stuffed teddy bear with loose button eyes and a stitched-on mouth, fashioned out of a piece of red felt, is propped up against the railing. Accompanying the bear is a baby's toy, made from a small gourd with a wooden handle attached by a strip of leather, and filled with dried black-eyed peas to make it rattle.

The excitement of a new child ended quickly; the reality of another son was bitter-sweet. A boy who would grow up big and strong to help his family on the farm, but this one had a deformity. Mary Ellen's father was hastily sent into town to get Dr. Foley. The midwives stayed, comforting the heart-stricken mother as best as they are able. It was a difficult situation and task. While cleaning her up, Haddy covers the mother with another quilt as Anne carries the soiled night dress and bed sheets to the back porch. She passes by Ben, sitting at the kitchen table, picking at a plate of biscuits with melting butter and dark maple syrup running down their sides. His grandmother is across from him mumbling into a cup of black coffee, while Mary Ellen stands by the crib looking at the baby. Haddy had earlier placed a delicate, lace scarf—almost as fragile as the moment—over the newborn's head to mask the cleft lip and palate. The baby lies on his back, crying between periods of snorting sounds caused by the severe opening between the roof of the mouth and the nasal cavity. His mother is curled up like a baby herself in the bed, crying, too. Mary Ellen tries to comfort her new little brother with one of her rag-dolls, gently shaking it over the crib. She is oddly not disturbed by his obvious deformity. She just wants him to stop crying.

"Mommy, the baby's crying. Can't you hear the baby? He's hungry. Mommy, feed the baby," she calls out.

Her mother continues to cry.

Anne walks over to Mary Ellen, crouching down close to her as she benevolently puts her arm around the little girl's waist.

"Why don't you take Ben outside and play?" she speaks softly in her ear.

"But I want to play with the baby."

"I know, dear, but he needs to rest."

"Okay."

She reluctantly places the rag doll next to the stuffed bear before joining Ben and their grandmother in the kitchen. Moments later the backdoor squeaks open and then the screen door slams as the children exit the house. But they do not play. Mary Ellen knows something is wrong, as does Ben who has said very little since the birth of the baby. They stand side by side looking back into the house through the screen door. A sudden chill in the October air makes Mary Ellen shiver. Their grandmother continues her mumbling at the table over her almost empty cup of coffee; almost as empty as the moment.

Moments later, their father's truck pulls back in front of the house, followed by a green, two-door Packard with Doctor Foley and his wife, Martha. The doors of the truck and those of the car open quickly, then all slam shut in unison. Once again the commotion of doors opening and closing and of footsteps scurrying on wooden floors fills the house.

Doctor Foley and his wife enter through the door first. They give a stiff nod of greeting to the midwives who are now standing by the crib. Haddy's eyes meet the doctor's as she returns a solemn nod. Anne subtly shakes her head at Martha. Mary Ellen's father removes his hat and stands rigid in the corner across the room.

Doctor Foley and the midwives hover around the baby, talking in whispers. Mrs. Foley walks over to the bed and sits down beside Mrs. Rushing, whose back is to the room.

"Farris, we're here for you. The doctor and I," she says in a comforting tone.

Mrs. Rushing lets out a string of sniffles.

"My baby is a monster."

Mrs. Foley rubs the anguished mother's back.

"Now, now, Dear. Now, now. You just try to rest."

Doctor Foley examines the newborn. Mary Ellen's grandmother remains at the table even though she heard the return of her son with the doctor and his wife. She already knows the outcome is not going to be a good one, but listens intently to their low voices. After sitting for a while longer, she slowly gets up and walks to the doorway. Her long gray hair, usually in a bun and neatly covered by a bonnet, is stringing out from the sides and the back.

Mary Ellen's father is in shock as he continues to stand in the corner, rooted to the floor like the cotton plants out in the fields. And, like the plants, he has been picked clean of any hope for his newborn by the obvious negative mood in the air. His eyes are wet from his earlier, silent cries of fear in the truck as he fetched the doctor, but he knows he can not show any emotion now. He keeps it contained inside, not allowing any signs of it to escape his hard, wooden exterior. Mary Ellen, with Ben in-tow, is standing to the side outside at the door of the front porch, both having crept around the house like curious cats. She sees her grandmother in the kitchen doorway through the screen and a streak of fear rushes through her.

Dr. Foley walks over to the distressed father. He reaches up to put his hand on his boulder of a shoulder. The doctor is much shorter, but his position as a physician makes him appear to stand ten feet tall. He removes his glasses with his free hand.

"It doesn't look good, Donald. The baby has a very pronounced deformity."

"Can't you help him?"

"I've seen this before, but not to this extent," the doctor continues.

The baby has stopped crying for the moment. Mary Ellen's father looks toward the crib and then turns his head, as his body remains unbending as he looks at his wife curled up on the bed. A strong wind rushes through the house, kicking the front screen door open. Mary Ellen jumps in response to the resulting slam.

Dr. Foley walks over to console the mother before consulting with Haddy again.

"You'll have to try to feed the baby with a spoon. Put a little cow's milk in it and gently pour it in his mouth. The baby will not be able to suckle from the mother," he tells the midwife.

Paul Dean starts crying again, but not like a normal newborn. The sounds are low and bubbly with an occasional loud burst. As the crying quiets, his breaths sound like a cat in distress.

"Yes, Doctor. I understand," Haddy responds.

"Sit the baby up in your lap; otherwise the milk will go into his nasal cavity."

Mary Ellen listens to every word the doctor says.

Dr. Foley walks a few steps back to the distressed father.

"If you can get the baby to Atlanta, something might be done. I'll see what I can do, but it will be costly. Until then, try to keep the mother calm and the baby from choking on the milk."

Mary Ellen's father nods his head.

"Haddy and Anne will do all they can for the infant," the doctor reassures.

Understandably, the days to follow were difficult; several passing before Mary Ellen's mother could even look at Paul Dean without bursting into tears. Then, she tended to him between spells of depression. Most of the care, though, was given by Grandmother Rushing and her granddaughter, when the midwives were not around. Mary Ellen eagerly attended to her new little brother, even staying home from school. It was a sacrifice she was willing to make.

The days since Paul Dean's birth rolled into weeks as a cheerless October was ripped from the calendar and the cold days of November quickly flipped by like turning the pages of a book. The days were growing shorter and shorter as Paul Dean's low cries fill the farmhouse. His father is busy around the farm getting ready for the winter months that are steadily marching closer. There is more wood to chop and stack to keep the fireplace and wood-burning stove hot, and food as well as other supplies to collect and store for the winter reserve.

As she has done often, Mary Ellen sits in the rocking chair next to the fire place with Paul Dean in her lap, trying to feed him. Outside the sun is low in the ginger-colored sky. Within the hour it will disappear and there will only be blackness surrounding the farmhouse. Ben is popping corn kernels in a metal wire basket to make popcorn balls as sweet potatoes roast in the ashes of the fireplace. Molasses is cooking on the stove for the popcorn. Collectively, they make the house smell sweet and smoky. Their mother and grandmother are sitting at the kitchen table, exhausted from long hours and lost hope; the last few days have been tough on the baby and the family. Mary Ellen dips the spoon into a bowl of milk on the side table and gently easies it through the opening of the baby's mouth. Softly and in a sweet young voice she recites a nursery rhyme.

"Rock a bye baby on the treetop, when the wind blows the cradle will rock..."

Sadly, he can not hear a word of it. It has been determined that Paul Dean is stone deaf. But she talks to him anyway. Since his birth, Dr. Foley has been by weekly and the midwives every few days. On the third week, the doctor noticed that Paul Dean did not react to the sound of the screen door slamming. He took a metal pan and hit it repeatedly with a spoon over the crib with no response from the infant. It is also apparent he has not gained any weight, and he weighs less than when he was born. As careful as everyone has been in feeding the baby, he has had bouts of choking as the milk aspirates into his lungs. Paul Dean's eyes are sunken and he is as white as the very cotton picked from the fields.

Mary Ellen concentrates on Paul Dean's deep blue

eyes, thinking how beautiful they are, and not on his deformed mouth or ailing appearance. They are so similar to Ben's, she thinks, almond in shape, but he has her chin and curly hair. All the children look like their mother. His tiny, delicate fingers grip Mary Ellen's. It is a calm moment—one of the few. The baby seems content in her lap; perhaps he feels safe. She is concerned for him, having overheard the doctor and the midwives on several occasions. And she has heard her father and grandmother talking while her mother was asleep, too. She knows there is a chance that the baby may die if he does not gain weight and continues to have choking spells. It was determined Paul Dean was too weak to make a trip to Atlanta and there was no money to pay for his care. Like most families in the country, the Rushings were still feeling the effects of The Great Depression of the 1930's and the Recession of 1937. Mary Ellen is careful to keep Paul Dean positioned properly in her lap like Anne had instructed. She loves her baby brother and wants him to be okay.

Her dog, Sadie, has been scratching and whimpering at the slightly ajar door, looking for Mary Ellen.

"I can't play now. I have to take care of Paul Dean."

Sadie sits at the door, her tail sweeping the porch.

"Ben, go play with Sadie," she tells her little brother.

"I will after Grandma and me make corn balls."

Ben hurries into the kitchen with the wire basket of steaming popped corn. Mary Ellen returns her attention to the baby. Sadie makes a low bark and runs off the porch and under the house. Mary Ellen's heart sinks in her chest for a moment. The memories of the puppies flood her mind. Her eyes tear up. The little puppies, she thinks to herself. Sadie's poor little puppies.

Mary Ellen found Sadie wandering on the farm when the dog was several months old. Just a baby like Paul Dean, she thinks to herself. Sadie was hurt, too, like her new little brother, limping up the dirt road when Mary Ellen was walking back from Folcome's Grocery one afternoon. The puppy was covered in cotton barbs, one deeply imbedded in her back paw. She carried the puppy home and begged her father to let her keep the puppy. At first he said no.

"We can't take care of that puppy, Child. Too much to do around here and we need all the food for us."

"But I will, Papa. I'll take care of her. Oh, Papa. Please let me keep her."

Reluctantly her father gave in to the innocent wishes of his daughter. Mary Ellen nursed the puppy back to health. Now, she is doing the same for Paul Dean, convinced she can fix him and make him well. For the first few months, Sadie lived in a box in Mary Ellen's room. As the puppy got bigger she lived under the house and was fed scraps from the table, meager ones at best. But Mary Ellen managed to sneak out more for her Sadie. They were inseparable. As the dog got older, Sadie would chase after the school bus for at least a quarter of a mile before giving up. And she would, without fail, be waiting for Mary Ellen in the afternoon to get home from school at the very spot the bus stopped to let her off. Then, the next spring, one afternoon, Sadie was not waiting for Mary Ellen when she got off the bus. The faithful dog had disappeared. For several days, Mary Ellen was understandably heart-sick, thinking she would never see the beloved pet again. Then, one day, like a miracle, there Sadie was, waiting for Mary Ellen to get off the bus. It was a joyous reunion. One of Mary Ellen's most treasured moments in her life—the return of her beloved Sadie.

About nine weeks later, Sadie had a litter of six puppies under the house. And more mouths to feed. At least that is how her grandmother saw them.

"No, Grandma, you can't take them from her," Mary Ellen pleaded, both she and Ben crying.

"Your father agrees. There are too many mouths to feed."

"But, we'll find them homes."

"No one around here wants another mouth to feed."

With the last word said, Grandmother Rushing puts the puppies in a box and takes them to the side of the house. Sadie is snarling and barking after her.

"Child, take your dog away from me," her grandmother commands.

Still crying, Mary Ellen holds Sadie around her neck. Her grandmother puts the box down by the black walnut tree. Then, one by one, she grabs the puppies, as they wiggle and yap in her hand. Quickly, she smashes their little heads downward against the large exposed roots of the tree, crushing their skulls. Mary Ellen turns her head in horror. She feels helpless as her knees give out from under her and she falls to the ground. She sobs, still holding on tightly to Sadie. Ben runs off under the house. In less than a minute, the puppies are dead.

"It's for the best, Child. It's for the best," says Grandmother Rushing.

She fills the box back up with the dead puppies and carries them across the road to the barn. Grandmother Rushing grabs a shovel and walks down the path deep into the woods. Mary Ellen never trusted her again.

Unfortunately, this was a common act on farms and in rural areas. Unwanted puppies were killed, either by this manner or, by putting them in seed or flour sacks weighted down with rocks and tossed into the river or pond. There was just not enough food to feed them or to run the risk of the females maturing and getting pregnant.

Paul Dean starts to choke again. Mary Ellen pulls the spoon out of his mouth and raises his head a little higher. He still continues to choke. She rocks him on her lap. The choking stops. She looks into Paul Dean's eyes as she rubs his little head.

"It's okay. It's okay," she tells him.

She continues with her nursery rhyme.

"When the bough breaks the cradle will fall, and down will come baby, cradle and all."

Mary Ellen is convinced her little brother is smiling, but it is hard to tell with the deformity. She sees it in his eyes—the smiling.

Grandmother Rushing gets up from the table to check the molasses while Ben eagerly stands by. She dumps the basket of popped corn into a large metal bowl, drizzling the hot molasses over the top and mixing it all together with a wooden spoon. Then she takes one handful after another of the sticky concoction, packing them into the shape and size of baseballs. Ben grabs one from the table before it has a chance to cool. He runs with it out the back door to find Sadie.

Mary Ellen's mother comes into the front room with one of the treats for her daughter.

"Why don't you take this and go join Ben, and put on your coat," she tells her daughter.

"Okay," Mary Ellen answers.

"But don't be gone too long. It's dark," her mother

insists.

She takes Paul Dean and sits down in the rocker. She feels numb inside for herself and the baby.

Mary Ellen runs out the door, almost running into her father as he is entering. She continues down the steps where she finds Sadie jumping up on Ben, trying to get the sweet cornball he has half eaten.

Their father stops for a moment in front of the fire to warm off the night's chill. He looks at his wife and she looks up at him, but they do not speak. Their eyes do that for them. He walks into the kitchen, grabbing a metal cup from the shelf to the side of the stove, filling it with coffee, before taking a seat at the table across from his mother. The house is quiet except for the sounds of the crackling fire and the squeaking floor under the rocking chair as Mrs. Rushing tries to sooth her son. Mary Ellen's mother leans her head back, listening to the conversation between her husband and mother-in-law.

"It has to be done," she hears her mother-in-law.

"I don't know."

The conversation becomes hushed whisperings with an occasional outburst.

"Yes. There is no other choice."

"No. No."

From where she is sitting, she can see the back of her mother-in-law through the kitchen doorway, but her husband is out of her sight-line. She continues to rock the baby, uncertain of what is to come.

There are more whispers.

"But, he's my son."

She hears the chair under her husband quickly slide back from the table as it scrapes the floor. Then his heavy boot steps out the kitchen door.

Nursery Rhymes

As the evening hours mature, Paul Dean has fallen asleep in his mother's arms. She continues to gently rock him by the fire. Mary Ellen and Ben have come back into the house and are getting ready for bed. Their father had gone to the barn when he left the kitchen. His wife can see the oil lantern glowing from across the road.

She hears her mother-in-law exit the back door and her footsteps going around the house. Moments later, through the window, she catches a glimpse of her frail frame, with back slightly hunched over, crossing the road and entering the barn.

Mary Ellen joins her mother in the front room.

"Momma, do you want me to hold him for you?"

"It's past time for you to get to bed," she answers.

But Mary Ellen does not want to go to bed. She wants to rock Paul Dean and sing nursery rhymes to him some more, but she can tell her mother is serious. Mary Ellen looks Paul Dean in the eyes, giving him a smile and then kisses him on his little forehead. She walks toward her bedroom, then stops halfway and looks back before going through the door and to bed.

Her mother sees her mother-in-law crossing back over the road to the house. She enters the front door. A blast of cold air fills the room.

"Let me take the baby. You go on to bed."

"Okay, I'm tired."

"I know, we all are."

She stands up. Her mother-in-law reaches for Paul Dean and sits down in the rocker. Mrs. Rushing remains there for a moment in front of the fire, then walks over and lies down in the bed. Mary Ellen's grandmother begins slowly rocking the baby back and forth, back and forth looking off in the distance. She starts mumbling

something. Mary Ellen had heard her grandmother returning. She gets out of bed and stands in the doorway watching unnoticed for a moment. Then her eyes meet her
grandmother's.

"Go on to bed, Child. And close the door."

Mary Ellen does not move at first. She looks harder at
her grandmother.

"Do I need to take a switch to you?"

Mary Ellen warily takes a step backwards. She puts
her hand on the door, pushing it closed in slow motion
until it shuts. A swell of uneasiness fills her body as she
climbs back into bed. She is afraid, but not quite sure of
what.

Another morning has come after a long night. It is
Thanksgiving Day. Outside the November air feels like
ice. A snowy frost is on the ground for the third morning
in a row. White-gray clouds hang low, suffocating the
soon-approaching blue-wintry sky from view. Inside the
house, the flames are burning low in the fireplace. Grandmother Rushing, pale and drained from being up all night,
throws a few more logs on. The blaze quickly kicks up,
chasing the chill out of the room. But it is not enough to
warm her.

Mary Ellen stumbles out of bed, rubbing the sleep
from her eyes. The wooden floor is cold under her feet.
She opens the door leading to the front room. Habitually
she walks in the direction of the crib. At first glance it is
gone. She thinks her eyes are playing tricks on her. In
confusion and disbelief she rubs them more before looking again. The crib is indeed gone. She surveys the room
and then swallows the breath in her mouth.

Her father is standing by the window. She runs to him.

"Papa, Papa," she starts to cry. "Where is the baby?"

He motions across the room on the bed. Mary Ellen looks in the direction of her father's eyes to see Paul Dean's body wrapped up in a bundle. His head is covered up, too. Tears run down her cheeks.

"Shhhh, Child. He's gone to heaven," her father answers with a huge lump of sadness in his throat.

Mrs. Rushing is in the kitchen. Her eyes are puffy and fiery red as she stands with her back to the stove. Mary Ellen looks at her grandmother standing emotionless in front of the fireplace. She then tries to catch her breath. She knows without having to ask, and her grandmother knows she knows as well. Mary Ellen takes several steps backwards before turning and running into her room.

By noon, a small white casket with the paint still tacky, delivered mid-morning, sits on a wooden table in front of the window where the crib had been. Inside, a brown, furry, stuffed teddy bear with loose-button eyes and a stitched-on-mouth fashioned out of a piece of red felt lies next to Paul Dean's little body as does the rattle and one of Mary Ellen's rag dolls. A thin piece of white lace covers his face. Mary Ellen's mother and father sit in chairs next to the casket.

Neighbors from the surrounding farms have been covering the kitchen table with plates of food since late morning. Included are a small ham from the midwives and a turkey from Dr. Foley and his wife—all the customary food for a family to fill their bellies with thanks and gratefulness. But there will be no celebration today. No hunger, except that of loss turning in their bellies.

During the night, after Mary Ellen, Ben and their mother fell asleep, Grandmother Rushing smothered Paul Dean with a pillow. She most likely believed it was the merciful thing to do. He was deformed, deaf, weak and growing weaker. Like any other animal on the farm, only the strong can survive.

Uncle Ben drove to the old graveyard on the way back to the house. I stood, humbled, in front of the headstones of my grandparents, my great-grandmother, and the simple, weathered, flat, rectangle marker on Paul Dean's grave; well settled into the ground. The inscription read:

Paul Dean
Son of Donald & Farris Rushing
October 9, 1939 – November 23, 1939

Holding On

It was raining outside. A sluggish, warm drizzle fell out of a late-summer sky. My mother was sitting on the edge of her bed, simply dressed in a pair of bright, green slacks and a cream blouse. Her hair was casually brushed back and her face void of makeup. Her skin, pale and her eyes blank. The only jewelry she had on was her wedding band. She was medicated and had been drinking. Her overnight bag was packed on the floor just inside the bedroom door. I was twelve years old, sitting in the chair by the rain-splattered window across from the bed. My father was drinking a beer in the living room, angry. The week before, he had taken off work to take care of my sister, brother and me while Mother lay in bed most of the time.

They both had been drinking a lot and fighting during the weeks before. There were bruises—like finger prints—on her arms where he had repeatedly grabbed and shaken her, trying to shake the crazy out of her body. A gray shadow—a remnant from a previous fight several weeks prior—was visible under her right eye. He said it was her fault that he got mad and hit her, that if she would just straighten up it would not have happened. I did not believe him. I knew it was not her fault. She was going back into the hospital for a "rest" and to get her medications sorted out, our father had told us. She had earlier been diagnosed as bipolar. I had witnessed her roller coaster periods of depression and manic episodes, but at the time I was too young to understand. I just knew there was something profoundly wrong with her. I knew she was very sad and lonely.

My Uncle Ben left the day before. He came to take her back to Fayette, but she would not go without us—her children—and he could not take us, too. He was married and had his own children. I wanted her to go. I wanted her to leave us. I wanted her to get away from my father. At the time, I wondered if my uncle hated my father as much as I did, and I wondered if he believed my father's story that she had gotten the bruises from constantly falling down drunk. Sometimes I think my uncle was unsure of whom to believe. One moment she was screaming at the top of her lungs like a cornered, wild animal and the next she was weeping like an innocent, lost child. Uncle Ben talked to her for hours while our father made us stay outside. From under the large magnolia tree, ornamented with white flowers, I could see my mother standing at the jalousie windows of the breakfast room looking at the large, regal blossoms as my uncle stood behind her with his arm on her shoulder, their mouths moving and their heads shaking. I prayed he could convince her to leave.

The dreary weather could not have been any more fitting for what was going on inside. I continued to watch Mother sitting unresponsive—almost lifeless—on the bed, appearing helpless. Then, I would look outside at the rain falling sluggishly over the day. I could tell she was worried and crying on the inside just as it was outside. A slow, constant cry. She was carefully holding a black-and-white picture by its white-trimmed scalloped edge; earlier, she had pulled it out of an envelope from a box on the top shelf of the closet. She had been holding it in her hand for a long time, her gaze unchanging. I had seen the picture before and she had told me the story behind it on many occasions with great delight, like a bedtime tale. It was a happy story and her face lit up every time she relived it. Her eyes were as big as apples and her smile was tremendous. The picture is of her and Gene Autry, the Country Western singer and actor, taken in the mid 1940's outside The Richard's Theater in Fayette, Alabama. They are standing under the massive marquee. He is wearing a double-breasted suit, a large cowboy hat and pointy boots. She is eighteen, looking sweet and excited and all dressed up—nothing like I would imagine a farm girl would look like. Accompanying the picture is her official Gene Autry Fan Club membership card.

Two years earlier, before the picture was taken, Mary Ellen and her first cousin, Sue, took a bus to see him perform in a road show in Birmingham.

"I was such a groupie back then," my mother laughed, retelling the story in years past.

I would smile at the glee in her voice.

"I found out what hotel he was staying at...and got his room number by flirting with one of the young bellmen.

Sue was standing behind me, nervous, saying we were going to get kicked out of the hotel. I walked right up to his room and knocked on the door, jittery as a chicken staring at a hungry fox on the other side of the pen, when it opened and he—the great man himself—was standing in front of me. I didn't know what to say. I had not thought I would get that far…my mouth must have gaped open for a minute or so. Sue gasped."

"What did he do?" I asked.

"Well, somehow I finally got my wits about me and said, 'Oh! It's you, Mr. Autry. I'm your biggest fan and I want to be a singer one day, too.' "

"What did he say?"

"He smiled big and invited us to join him in the tea room of the hotel."

"Really?"

"Yes, really," Mother giggled like she was sixteen again.

Well, apparently Gene Autry was so delighted with Mary Ellen that he spent the afternoon at the fairgrounds before the show with her and Sue. Then he took them to the theater. Mother went on to tell me that before the show, he took her on stage and asked her if she knew any of his songs.

" 'Are you kidding!' I asked Mr. Autry," Mother explained.

I laughed.

"He picked up his guitar and started playing a tune. 'If you know the words, just join in,' he challenged me. Well, of course I knew the song and joined in and belted it out. Sue stood off to the side with this silly, amazed look on her face as I sung a duet with Mr. Gene Autry, himself."

When he came to Fayette two years later to do a show,

Mother took her little brother to see him. Uncle Ben recalled the event as I sat at the kitchen table when I went back to visit after my mother had passed away. As he retold the story, they had gotten to the theater early.

"Your mother must have spent hours getting ready. She was a pretty amazing looking girl. She had been excited for weeks before the show. Well, your mother took me backstage, like she owned the place, to see if she could find Mr. Autry."

Uncle Ben went on to tell me that they were soon stopped by a big, burly stagehand, asking what they were doing.

"Well, your mother straightened her shoulders and calmly told him she was a friend of Mr. Autry. And, at the very moment she was being questioned, I saw a pair of large cowboy boots coming down the stairs."

"What happened next?" I asked.

"Then the stagehand turned and asked Mr. Autry if he knew this pretty, young lady."

"And?"

"Well, all I remember is staring at those big boots and at his oversized cowboy hat to match, and then this big voice came out of the man: 'Why, Mary Ellen. So good to see you.'"

My uncle went on to tell me how the smile on Mother's face exploded when Gene Autry remembered her.

"Your mother smiled from ear to ear. She then introduced me and, after a few minutes of conversation, another man came over to tell Mr. Autry he had to get ready for the show. Mary Ellen politely started to excuse us to find our seats, but to her surprise Mr. Autry asked us to stay backstage to watch the show."

From hearing the story over and over, I knew sitting there on that rainy summer day, across from my mother, that that picture meant everything to her. It represented all her hopes and dreams as a young girl. And for the time she was sitting there holding the picture, she had taken herself back in her mind all those years and years, and was reliving the experiences with Gene Autry. Remembering what it felt like to stand on a big stage and sing a song with him. Remembering what it was like to have big dreams and, for a while, believe that one day they would come true. Now, she was fearful of losing the picture and the membership card, fearful of losing those very hopes and dreams, fearful that it would be lost if she took it with her and destroyed if she left it behind. It was the only evidence that the event had actually happened, that at one time, for a very brief period, she was happy.

Her history of electroshock therapy had impaired her recent memories before and after the treatments, and I think she was also fearful that any new treatments would wipe out the memories she so desperately wanted to hold on to. Most patients had side effects such as struggling to recall the memory of events of a period of time before and after the treatments, but very few patients had long-term effects or lost memories as far back as childhood. I believe my mother still feared the possible destruction of those memories so dear to her. The treasured photo and the fan club card were the only things left that she had to hold on to except for a few booklets of sheet music. Ever since my mother was a young girl, she had collected music. She sang like a song bird around the house, but mostly when my father was not there. She cherished every note on every page of music she had acquired over the years. Her angelic voice complemented her beauty. The music had been neatly stacked and cataloged in boxes of equal size and appearance—boxes and boxes—from classical to country to popular. While she had been in the hospital a previous time, recuperating from one of her breakdowns, in my father's anger he had collected the music and thrown the sheets out like useless trash. He had overlooked a few, which I hid from him. The destruction of her music sent her back into a depression when she discovered what he had done. Without her music, there was little for her to hold on to. She mourned its lost like the loss of a child.

The rain continued outside as it did in her soul. It was time to go. I heard my father walking down the hall with his keys rattling in his hand. He stopped in the doorway. Neither one of us looked up at him.

"I'm taking the bag to the car. It's time to go."

He picked it up and headed to the back door.

"Mommy, are you okay?" I asked.

She looked up at me.

"I'm okay if you're okay."

She put the picture back in the envelope and held it for another minute before getting up from the bed. Slowly she walked over to the desk. She opened the middle drawer and pulled out a roll of tape.

"You have to help me keep this safe. Can you do that?" she asked.

"Yes. What do you want me to do?"

She walked over to the dresser, reaching behind the small space just wide enough to fit her hand. She taped the envelope to the back of the attached mirror.

She addressed my reflection in the mirror.

"I just want you to remember where it is. Will you? Will you remember? And don't tell your father."

"I won't. I'll never tell him."

My mother's dreams were a big part of who she was. Seeded in childhood, ideas of what she wanted out of life: a career; places to travel; sunsets to watch over distant oceans; open fields to run free in; mountains to climb to the top; someone to support and understand her; someone's hand to hold as she grew older. From a very early age they sprouted inside of her—those dreams. As Mary Ellen transformed from a little girl into a young woman, their roots entangled and cocooned her heart and became tied to the one thing that kept her alive later in life when she had lost so much of herself: hope. Earlier on, those dreams were her friend, but gradually they become her enemy. She held on to them for many years, but eventually watched them slipping away. Finally, she had to let them go, but not without a fight. The last ten years of my mother's life, I watched her reluctantly let go of those dreams and settle for some relief from the constant ache inside of her soul and for a quiet place to rest as she grieved their loss.

My mother opened the top drawer of the dresser. She removed her wedding band, laid it inside and closed the drawer.

"Come, walk me to the door."

I stood up and walked over to her. She reached out her hand as she slightly staggered backward.

"I'll be okay. Don't you worry," she said, as she ran her other hand over my head.

Love Letters & Broken Promises

One day she was a little girl working in the fields filling sacks with cotton, the next she was living on her own, and, before she knew it, she was married to a man she barely knew—my father. Before him and since leaving the farm, she had scarcely had time to be a carefree young woman. Mary Ellen had little experience with men except for a few, innocent school-girl romances like Dexter, who gave Mother her first friendship ring made out of the material used in the construction of fake gums. The setting was a tooth. He had a part-time job making dentures and, apparently, a humorous side, but she was not very amused or impressed by the jester, and gave it to her brother. It was a short romance.

Mother's next love interest, Frank, was from a well-to-do family with one of the largest farms in the county. He stood her up on one of their early dates because his pet hog was giving birth. That was the last of Frank. There were others, too, who showed interest in her; that is what some of Mother's childhood friends told me. "All the rich boys liked your mother. She was such a pretty girl. But she was a 'good girl' and many of them were just interested in things that good girls don't do." Raymond was a few years older and stood out over the rest, a storybook prince charming, tall with dark curly hair. "A handsome boy," my uncle told me. "I believe your mother really liked him the best of all her suitors. She was seventeen, if I remember correctly, when he went off to the War. His body was never found. Mary Ellen was heartbroken. She didn't come out of her room for days and days after she got the news he was missing."

My mother met my father on a blind date. Mary Ellen was twenty years old and working at the County Extension Office in Fayette. A few years prior, just days after graduating from high school, she moved out of the four-room farmhouse into town, leaving the dirt road for the paved streets. Mary Ellen was able to get out on her own from the money she had saved while working at Scott's. She rented a room in a large house from Mr. and Mrs. Dobbs just a few blocks from the main drag, Timble Avenue, which ran north and south through Fayette. It was an uncertain time, but she was finally off the farm and away from the cotton fields where she had spent endless hours picking and bagging the Alabama Snow. She had always had a plan and now it was just beginning to unfold. Mary Ellen wanted to go to college, but it was not an option at the time. Instead, she would work to make money and practice her singing.

Downtown Fayette was a far cry from the big-city life she dreamed of, but at least it was a start. Like most rural towns, it orbited around the city hall, a Greek-influenced building. There was a theater, The Richard's, where Mary Ellen spent many hours as a young girl captivated by her favorite movie stars; fueling her own dreams of becoming a singer and, possibly, an actress. Going to the movies was an event and an escape from the farm. Back then, a ticket cost only fifty cents; a small price to pay for an afternoon or evening of dreaming. And, after she moved into town, it was only a few blocks away from her door, as everything was in walking distance of the Dobbs' home. Mary Ellen no longer had to wait for a ride into town in the back of a pick-up truck. Hodges' Department Store was four blocks south, where she would window shop the latest fashions inspired by New York City and Paris. The Curb Market was two blocks west, where she purchased fresh vegetables and fruit when the supply her parents shared from their garden ran out.

My father, Woody, was from Chapel Hill, Tennessee. He dropped out of high school in 1942 to join the Army, lying about his age to get in at the midpoint of World War II. While in boot camp in Columbus, Georgia, he became friends with a local Fayette boy, Buzz Sawyer, whose girlfriend, Ruth, was best friends with my mother. Several years later, World War II ended and the Korean War was at its peak. While on leave after a tour, Woody came to town to visit Buzz. Ruth thought it would be a good idea to fix her best friend up so they could double date. Although my mother had gone on a few dates with John Holmes, a young lawyer from Tuscaloosa, she agreed to meet at Scott's for a quick bite to eat and later, catch a movie at The Richard's Theater.

Scott's was the place to be on a Saturday night in Fayette, Alabama. In fact, it was the only place to be. Ruth and Mary Ellen were sitting at a booth having a soda when Buzz and Woody arrived. My mother was instantly taken in by her blind date's rugged physique and dark, good looks. She noticed an uncanny resemblance to Richard Egan, the movie star. After seeing him in his first movie, *The Story of Molly X*, she had developed a huge crush on the actor. In fact, she was so taken by Egan that she wrote the studio a letter to find out about becoming a member of his fan club. The studio passed the letter on to him, and a few months later she received a hand-written reply with an autographed picture.

> *Dear Mary Ellen,*
> *I don't have a fan club yet, but I appreciate your interest in me and my work. How would you like to be president and start one up?*
> *Fondly,*
> *Richard Egan*

My father ended up spending all of his leave in Fayette, and Mother never went out with John, the lawyer, again. Their courtship lasted a few months. Then, on Saturday afternoon, September 27, 1952, Woody dressed in his Army uniform and picked Mother up at the Dobbs' home. She was standing on the front veranda in a white scooped-neck dress with delicate lace on the sleeves. A single strand of pearls, borrowed from Ruth, showed off the swan-like curve of her neck and its delicate, smooth skin. They were on their way to get married. There was a waiting period in Alabama, so instead they drove forty-three miles across the state line to Columbus, Mississippi, where no waiting was required. Mary Ellen told only Ruth and Buzz about the pending nuptials. Weeks later when she did tell her parents, they were extremely disappointed. They thought a young lawyer was a better choice than a high school dropout. But Mary Ellen was head-over-heals and desperate to get out of Fayette. Woody's movie star good-looks and promises had swept her off her feet. His next station was to be in France and Mary Ellen wanted to see Paris.

They were married for twenty-two years. A relationship that started out with joy and excitement ended in horror. With such a conclusion, it is hard to believe my parents were ever in love, but I know that at one time they were. Perhaps it was a misguided love, but all the same it was love. I know there was a moment in their lives when they first stared into each others' eyes and saw what love looked like, and then tasted it with their lips. Surely, early on, in the beginning, they had experienced such a moment before their relationship turned turbulent, fell into chaos, and my father tasted the cold steel of a rifle.

The proof is written in notes and on the back of pictures they sent to each other. Although they lost and eventually forgot those moments of confessed love, their writings are reminders of two hearts that once longed to be together. One such note is written behind one of my favorite pictures of Mother sitting today on my desk in a 4-inch -by-4-inch simple black marble frame with delicate white veins. In the black and white image, she is with child, dressed in maternity attire. She is carrying my older brother in her swollen belly. She was carrying life, creating it, and now life has left her. In the picture, her smile boarders on glee, so I know there must be joy behind her lips, very unlike the rare smiles that crossed her face later in life, always with a curl of sorrow at the corners. The writing on the back is concealed and held in secret by the frame. The message is simple, but as endearing as it is tender. Her penmanship is perfect and in straight lines, its lettering, somewhat taut and evenly spaced.

Darling,
This jacket makes me appear larger than I really am.

I Love you,
Mary Ellen

She had sent it to my father who was stationed overseas at that time. I wonder what must have gone through his mind as he pulled it from the envelope, perhaps scented with her perfume, and gazed at her image. Did an expansive smile explode on his face? Did his heart beat more rapidly as he read her uncomplicated loving note on the back? Was he proud to have her and know she belonged to him? Did he read it over and over before putting it in the pocket next to his heart? Did he yearn to be close to her again? I wonder when the last time was that she called him "darling," before their love was choked by the hostility that raged sporadically in a house suffocated by the smoke of an uncertain rage; and her body—time and time again—was marked by his cruel hand that left her bruised and broken, mentally as well as physically.

I often wonder what happened between them. When did they stop looking at each other and see hate instead of love? As a young child I do remember moments when they seemed happy. My father was strong and handsome. My mother loved his black hair and compelling, blue eyes and he loved her angelic beauty and smooth, even skin.

She would sit on his lap in the beige recliner in the living room as she ran her fingers through his hair. He had his arm wrapped around her curvy waist, nuzzling his nose into her side. "I'm the luckiest man in the world to have such a beautiful woman," he would tell us, and then take a swig of his beer before passing it to her. They would laugh as my sister, brother and I just giggled at them—as little kids do—from our seats on the sofa, too young to understand why they were acting so silly. But we were happy as long as they appeared happy. They would laugh and drink, and Mother would make our father's favorite meal of fried oysters and cole slaw, from scratch of course. She would fix him up a plate and return to his lap, feeding him.

As good as it could get, it could go in the opposite direction—fast! There are times when I remember through the eyes of a little boy. I find myself back in my room in that house, its outer walls hiding from the outside world what was happening on the inside. It was night. I was perched in my bed on my knees as I looked from the dark room into the hallway lit by the single light over the mirror-covered medicine cabinet; my line of sight in direct view of the bathroom across the hall. One second the house was silent and the next, it erupted into pandemonium by slamming doors and my parents' yelling voices.

"I'll kill myself if you touch me," screamed my mother, as the silhouette of her nude body ran down the hallway.

"Mommy, Mommy," my sister called from her room.

"Stay in your room and go to sleep!" My father yelled back at her.

Sleep? How could anyone sleep? I remember thinking, as my brother lay in his bed across from mine, pretending to do so.

"Don't run from me, damn it!" yelled my father, also nude, as he pursued my mother.

I could hear my parents tussling in the kitchen. The sound of utensils spilling on the floor from a drawer pulled violently open off its tracks. Then, the sound of my mother's bare feet hitting the floor as she ran back up the hallway, the steel of a knife reflecting the light as she ran into the bathroom and slammed the door. The hallway quickly darkened except for a thin line of light seeping out between the threshold and the space at the bottom of the door.

"I told you if you touch me again I'll kill myself! I'll kill myself with this butcher knife!"

"Mary Ellen, unlock the damn door or I'll kick it in," my father yells, as he tries to force it open with brute force.

"Stay out of here!"

My father's body slams against the door, one, two, three times. It finally gives way to his force and the hallway explodes with light again, exposing their nude bodies struggling over the knife. My mother, holding it high above her head, its blade pointing downward toward her breasts and his chest. My father's hands around hers trying to take it. Both of them out of breath, breathing heavily and grunting as their bodies weakened from the struggle. At any moment, I expected the knife to plunge into one of them.

Feeling helpless and unable to look anymore, I closed my eyes and covered them with my hands. At that tender age, there were no more tears to cry. Suddenly, the knife clanged as it hit the linoleum floor. I opened my eyes just as they were each trying to reclaim it.

"Stop. Please stop!" I remember screaming.

They were so wrapped up in the madness that they had been unaware of my witnessing the chase and the struggle. They looked in my direction.

"Go to sleep, Randy!" my father called out, irritation in his voice.

He retreated to their bedroom. My mother went in the other direction toward the kitchen. In their embarrassment they had left the butcher knife where it had fallen from their struggle. I heard the bedroom door close behind my father. Moments later, my mother quietly walked back down the hallway and went into my sister's room. The door creaked open and then closed. Now the house was quiet again. My eyes focused on the knife discarded on the floor, fearful one of them would come back for it. A few minutes passed, which seemed like hours. I eased out of my bed, walking as carefully and quietly as possible in the direction of the bathroom. I stopped, standing over the knife. I felt the chill of the floor climb up my body from the soles of my bare feet to the back of my neck. Nervously I listened for my parents; my heart pounding in my chest as I warily leaned over to pick up the knife. I remember it feeling cold and heavy in my hand as I carried it back into my bedroom.

"What you doing?" Steven whispered, as he sat up in bed.

I did not answer him. I stood just inside the door looking around the room for a hiding place to put the knife so my parents could not find it. The reality that the kitchen drawers were full of knives did not occur to me. It was only important at that moment to hide this one. I slid the knife under the dresser as far as my stretched arm and extended fingers could reach. I crawled back into bed, pull-

165

ing the covers to my ears, listening to the silence, and guardedly watching the hallway lit by the light of the bathroom.

In the years to follow, my parents lived in the house like strangers avoiding each other. Toward the end, the fighting diminished. They passed each other in the hallway with few words spoken. In the days before his death, my father had been off on a drinking binge. On the night of his return, I was working at my part-time job as a short-order cook at the local Shoney's restaurant that my brother got me. Steven called to inform me our father was back, and he had been involved in a car wreck where he rear-ended a woman's car. I had only two fears: he was back and whose mother from school did he hit? It was sure to be a topic of conversation between classes the next day.

Upon my return home from work, my father was sleeping off his drunk on the living room sofa. His snores filled the house as I entered the back door. I was relieved he was asleep so I did not have to face him. I smelled the liquor from his heavy breathing as I passed through the kitchen which divided the living and dining rooms from the bedrooms.

The next morning, he was still in the living room. I could hear him stirring around from where I was standing in the kitchen waiting on my sister so we could leave for school. Our brother had already left, and our mother was sleeping in Sandra's room. My anger had not diminished from the night before, and I still feared possible embarrassment later at school if indeed he had hit a classmate's mother's car. Once my sister joined me in the kitchen, our father overheard our whispering. He called us into the living room. It was a pitiful call, unusually undemanding. I sternly shook my head "no" at my sister, but she went in to see him. I waited in the kitchen out of view for a few moments before angrily calling out to her.

"Hurry up! We're going to be late."

I left without saying goodbye to my father. A few hours later, he was dead.

Shortly after we had left, our father called a taxi to take him to a sporting goods store. There, he purchased a rifle and bullets while the taxi waited outside. When he came home, my father went to my parents' bedroom and placed all his government papers and financial documents on the desk in front of the large window facing the street. He made a list of people to call before going to the closet and removing his army uniform—wrapped in plastic from its last cleaning from years ago—out of retirement. Meticulously he laid it out with the medals from his military service, including his Purple Heart from the Korean War, on the bed my parents had not shared as husband and wife in many, many years. After he had finished, he went back to the living room where he had spent most of the previous night vomiting into a paper bag.

That fateful morning, they were alone in the house. From my sister's room, Mother heard a muffled shot reverberate through the house. At first she mistook it for the BB gun my father used in the backyard to keep the squirrels out of the fruit trees. Perplexed as to why he was shooting it in the house, she got out of bed to investigate. She put on her housecoat and slippers before heading down the hallway, then went cautiously through the kitchen until she stopped in the doorway leading to the dining room that was a level above the living area, divided by a long, four-foot wide brick planter filled with dusty, green plastic plants. It had been overcast all morning. The light in the house was spongy and made fragile by the se-

167

curely drawn curtains of the living and dining rooms. Mother's vision was indistinct as she took a step into the upper level of the dining room. Then she looked down to see her husband lying on the sofa, from the chest down, with what appeared to be a rifle lying on his chest, gripped in his hands. His face was hidden by the tall, large shade of the lamp on the end table. She called out to him.

"Woody. What are you doing?"

She heard him gurgle.

"Woody," she called out, again.

Mother stepped down. Her knees buckled out from under her at the sight of his face. She caught herself on the brick divider as she witnessed the blood running out of the back of his head, the rifle lodged in his mouth.

"Oh, Woody! What did you do?" she screamed out.

He was still alive when the ambulance arrived, choking on his blood. It would not be the quick death he had planned for himself. What life was left in his body rapidly drained out on the way to the hospital. My father was pronounced "Dead on Arrival" at the Warner Robins Air Force Base Medical Center.

My brother, sister and I were called out of our second period classes. Although the circumstances surrounding his suicide were beyond horrible, I still felt a sense of relief. His death was just another event in the lengthy list of bad things that was common in our lives. As was customary, I felt we had to act like everything was okay. We had to pick ourselves up and move forward.

My mother and sister were taken to a friend's home to be consoled. Steven and I returned to the house. The seasons had changed. It was Fall. Scores of colored leaves, discarded by the trees surrounding the house, swirled in the air as they fell to the ground, crackling under our feet as we questioningly approached the door. We pulled down the investigation tape left by the police, unsure of what we would find once inside. I felt uneasy walking back into the house after knowing what had taken place. Foreboding, we walked into the living room and stood over the sofa looking at what our father had left behind: the deep indention of his body in the sofa from sleeping there over years of estrangement from Mother, his spilled blood drained from his body saturating the fibers of the brown-and-green tweed-like fabric of the sofa and the forest-green thick-piled carpet, and bits of tissue ripped from his head by the speeding bullet. Minutes later, Steven took off in his car. I was left alone. The air smelled like death—sweet and thick. I held my breath as long as I could before running back outside, tripping down the stairs, to breathe again.

I stood in the center of the backyard and looked up at the treetops and beyond. Looking for God. It had been awhile since I had been to church, but at that moment I needed to believe in something, or someone. I needed to believe that God existed. The Fall leaves cascaded down around me as my whole body felt numb. I felt no emotion. If anything, perhaps, for a fleeting second, I felt sorry for my father. And if God did exist, then I would somehow get through this. All I knew was: I had to act like nothing out of the ordinary had taken place and clean up the mess and any evidence of the event before my mother returned. I breathed in deeply until my lungs were unable to hold anymore and walked back into the house. I got a bucket and sponge from the utility closet off the kitchen and squirted a large amount of dish soap into the bottom before filling it with hot water from the faucet. Bluish-white bubbles overflowed the top. I carried the steaming, sloshing bucket into the living room and got down on my hands and knees scrubbing as hard as I could to get the last remaining drops of my father out of the house once and for all. As I was cleaning, someone from the funeral home arrived. He told me that cold water works best. I flushed the red water from the bucket down the toilet. But it would take more than soap and water to remove Father from our lives. He saw to that. The permeating smell of death lingered in the house. Not long after his suicide, I begged my mother to sell, but she never would. Instead she chose to live—if it could be called living—in the house filled with his violence and now soaked in his blood.

Upon his departure from this world at his own hand, I was not suddenly overtaken by grief. I did not cry. The first thing I thought of after hearing he was dead was that my mother would have a new chance at life. Yes, a new life. I saw his death as the key that would unlock the chain in which he had shackled her spirit for many years. A small part of me rejoiced. Finally she was free, or at least I had hoped. I was naive. I soon learned that it would not be easy to break free of him, even though he was dead, and that in death—he would have a greater hold on her and on all of us.

A Chance for a New Beginning

After my father's death, I wanted her to marry again. I desperately wanted someone to love and adore my mother for the rest of her life. I wanted someone to bathe her in affection and hopefully drown out all the misery that my father had caused. I wanted someone to give her stability. I wanted someone to believe in her as I did—someone to believe she could overcome the past. And I wanted to be free to live my life without worrying about her. She was still beautiful and desirable, but the years of his abuse and disappointments had left her vacant inside. He had drained almost everything from her, and I feared it might be too late for her to regain any part of the woman she once was—the woman before his abuse.

My father had a twenty-thousand-dollar government life insurance policy, but Mother only received half because his death was a suicide. She also got a small annuity from his retirement; it was just enough to get by. There was no insurance on the house, so Mother had to find a job to pay the mortgage. My brother, sister and I each got one-thousand dollars. I stashed mine away to save for my move to California.

She did not have a lot of employment experience, so she took what she could get and what was in walking distance of the house. After she married my father, he never wanted her to work. She did work a few weeks in the lunchroom of Warner Robins High School, trying to get some independence, but my father beat her badly after she made the mistake of mentioning that one of the teachers had flirted with her. After that, she was unable to go back. My father's jealousy got the best of him, and of her, too. He did not want another man to take her from him. She was basically a hostage to her beauty and, therefore, to my father.

She had taken a job at a doughnut shop on Watson Boulevard about a quarter of a mile from the house. I remember her first day of work.

"How do I look, Son?" she asked, as small beads of perspiration collected above her lips.

She was standing in the breakfast room in a white uniform with black trim at the collar and on the ends of the short-sleeves. "Very pretty. You look really good."

"You sure?" she asked for more reassurance, patting her face with a folded tissue.

"Mom? Did you see yourself in the mirror? You look amazing."

And she did. Even in a donut shop uniform. It had been a long time since she had gotten all fixed up; not since Father's funeral, and then, an even longer time before that. Her make-up and hair looked perfect. She still had quite a figure. If only she believed she was pretty. She was still shaken up over the suicide so many months later. Sometimes I would catch her standing in the doorway of the kitchen, looking down into the living room. Just standing, doing the thing with her fingers and thumbs.

"Well, you ready to drop me off? Don't want to be late on my first day."

I followed her out the back door to the car. I hated that she had to get a job at this point in her life, but I saw it as a chance for her to get out of the house and, hopefully, meet someone.

"You sure I look okay, Son?"

"Mom! Elizabeth Taylor should be so pretty!" I said as I opened the car door for her.

Then, there was Eddie, the last man to love my mother, or the last one she allowed to know a part of her. He was a customer, and understandably quickly become smitten by Mother's beauty.

Eddie was a few inches taller than Mother. Good-looking, but not like my father was. Where my father had dark hair and light eyes, Eddie had blonde hair parted on the side and brown eyes looking through black, rectangular glasses. He frequently came into the donut shop in the afternoons after work. He sat at the end of counter and ordered the same thing: black coffee and two chocolate donuts with sprinkles. He started coming in more after my mother started working there. Her second week on the job he asked her out. She politely turned him down. But Eddie was persistent; a month later he came by the house to take Mother out to dinner.

"Are you sure I should go out with Eddie?" she nervously asked.

She was standing in the kitchen clipping on a pair of silver earrings as I was sitting at the kitchen table doing

Alabama Snow

my math homework.

"Yes. He sounds like a nice guy."

"But I think it's too soon."

"It'll do you good to have some fun."

"What shoes should I wear with this dress? Do you think these earrings go?"

Even back then I was her personal stylist. Since I was a little boy, she made me pin-curl her hair weekly.

"Definitely the black shoes with the open toes. And, yes, the earrings are perfect, Mother."

The first date turned into two, and then three. One afternoon I came home from class around four. I found Mother sitting at the kitchen table, humming, drinking a cup of coffee and puffing on a cigarette. She looked happy and there was a glow radiating from inside her I had not seen since I was a little boy. And, as far as I could tell, she had not had any alcohol in weeks. It was obvious Eddie had been there, but left not long before I had arrived. There was a second cup, almost empty, positioned close to where she was sitting, and a chair pulled close to her, telling me they had been sitting side by side. There were two different brands of cigarette butts in the ashtray. They started going out a few times a week. Mother seemed to be finding some happiness, or at least I was hopeful. Eddie appeared to be the nice man I had thought, and I wondered if he would be the one to help her forget. He even took her to work and picked her up when his schedule allowed. They tied up the telephone most evenings. Mother was like a teenage girl sitting on her bed and talking on the phone to the boy in school she had a crush on. There were giggles and whispers, but I had no idea of how passionate their relationship had grown until I found his love letters after she passed away. They tell the story bet-

174

ter than I ever could. They are the proof.

His first letter:

Dear Mary,

You have captured my mind, and heart. I am a captive audience by choice! I find myself thinking of you constantly. By writing this letter, I somehow feel closer to you. It's 8:15 and I'm waiting for you to get off work so I can take you home.

I hope you can learn to accept me, and love me. I know the strain is tremendous, and wish it were easier for you to relax with me. I feel that in time, you will be able to welcome me, and look forward to being with me! There is an invisible barrier between us, but I think it can be surmounted.

I want to tell you that I think you are a wonderful woman. I have a very high opinion of you, your ethics, and your morals, and I have a lot of respect for you. I think you are in doubt of this, but it is true. The things we did last night were acts of love and passion, but were not without understanding and consideration. I have tried to be attentive and compassionate. I want us to experience many things together, but I don't want to hurt you or force you to do things you are not ready to do. Please forgive me if at times I am too demanding. I offer no apology for wanting and desiring you, but I apologize if in fact I have been too crude and demanding.

You have made me very happy, woman!

I love you,
Eddie

The invisible barrier between them was her history and my father. A year had passed and it was clear they were falling in love. Then, one morning she broke the news to me.

"Eddie asked me to marry him last night at dinner," she told me.

"That's great, Mother!"

"I said no, or rather not now."

"You're kidding me. Right?" I was furious at her.

"Mother, but he loves you! I thought you loved him."

"I don't know. They're sending him to Turkey for fifteen months."

"Well, can you go with him?"

"No. I'm not ready."

"Do you think you'll ever be ready to get remarried?"

"I'm not sure. I think I want to take some classes. I've been reading some of your college text books."

"That's great, but you can take classes and still marry Eddie, you know."

"Perhaps."

"What did Eddie say when you turned him down?"

"That he would ask me again when he got back from Turkey."

At first he called her every week and wrote regularly. Then, after several months, the calls and letters became fewer and fewer. Although he promised his love was forever, she was left alone again; left alone in the house with her husband's ghost. She started drinking again and was back to her old habits of staying up all night sitting at the kitchen table listening to old music and walking the house until dawn.

It was not long after that my mother went back into the hospital. I came home from class to find her half-conscious on her bed. She was talking some undistinguishable garble. There was an empty pill bottle by the bed and an empty bottle of whisky in the kitchen sink. I called the ambulance. I do not know if the overdose was intentional. Her stomach was pumped at the emergency room.

Several months later, after the incident, a letter came.

Dear Mary,

You probably think I've forgotten you, but I haven't, and I figured I'd better write to you and tell you what's up!

Well, since my last letter, Turkey continues to be quite an experience to state it mildly. I haven't really had long to adjust yet, but on the basis of what I've seen so far, it seems to be fair. They have moved me around a lot. From what I've been told, I'll be here for a while longer. Of course, it's too soon to say where I'll be going when I leave here, but I expect to return to Robins. As soon as I hear anything in the way of assignment, I'll write and tell you.

What have you been up to? Are you going to school yet? I miss you and it seems like such a long time since we've seen each other!

Well, I've got to go for now. Write me soon, honey. I'm anxious to hear from you. Be good and take care of yourself.

Your Eddie

I often have wondered what would have happened if Eddie had not been sent to Turkey. My mother's life was full of "what-ifs." What-if Raymond had made it back from the war? What-if my father had never met Buzz Sawyer, the local Fayette boy? *What-if?*

A Fine Line

"I hate you. I wish I'd never married your father and you were never born!" she growled and walked out of the room.

The anger in her voice sliced my heart in half. I looked back down at the biology text in front of me on my desk. I began to read where I had left off before the interruption: *Plants are categorized into two basic types: vascular and nonvascular. Vascular plants are considered to be more advanced than nonvascular plants due to the fact they have evolved. . . .* "What," I thought to myself. I had lost my concentration. I pushed the book away and put my head down on the desk in its place. I had had enough of Mother's drinking, and it was getting worse. College was hard enough without her going "crazy" on me.

I did not feel like I fit in and I carried the same insecurities I had in high school up the scholarly steps of Mercer University. I felt trapped commuting four days a week between Warner Robins and Macon, as if I were confined inside a big bubble separating me from the rest of the world. Luckily there were no classes on Wednesdays. "Wonderful Wednesdays"—as they were called—were set aside as a day of study and religious reflection.

My classes were usually from 8 a.m. to 2:30 p.m. I was up early in the mornings for the thirty-minute car ride, then back home in the afternoons, unless I decided to stay in the library to study. It was the most peaceful place I could find. Then to Shoney's for work several evenings and most weekends. I had to keep telling myself I was doing this for Mother, to make her stronger, to make her happy, but I was miserable. I wanted to be someplace else. I wanted to be in California. While in college, my mother's episodes of schizophrenic behavior increased and were compounded by her bipolar disorder of extreme highs and bottomless lows. She was seeing a psychiatrist monthly in Macon. I would drive her to the appointments and pass the time in the waiting room dreaming of the day when I could move away. Hating my life; sometimes hating her and feeling nothing would ever change for the better, fearing I would never be able to leave. Other times I would sit in the car outside the office, looking forward, telling myself to go—just go.

I could hear my mother walking around the house talking to herself, as usual. Every few minutes, the sound of her cigarette lighter flicking on and off filled the house until she got the cigarette lit. It seemed like she chain-smoked from the moment she woke up until the time she went to bed. The echoing pop of the opening of a can of beer followed. She had finished the bottle of whiskey I had watered down, but there was nothing I could do about the beer; and I was sure there was another bottle hidden somewhere in the house. Sometimes it was like a game of Hide-and-Seek. She would find new places to stash the booze and I would search them out. There were times when enough was enough and I would empty the whiskey in the kitchen sink with her screaming and fighting me to take the bottle back. She would barely be able to stand, with a facial expression of disbelief as if I were pouring out the last drops of a drug she desperately needed to stay alive. She just looked for better places to hide the bottles.

Like a big boil, it was all coming to a head; the infection that had been building up inside of me for so long. I prayed she would get tired and stop storming into my room; stop yelling how horrible my dead father was and how she had wasted her life. Or, as on previous occasions, stop bursting in demanding I take her to the liquor store so she could get more booze and cigarettes. If I refused to take her, she would just call Frank, her regular taxi driver, to either pick her up or just go by the liquor store and get her usual order. Sometimes it would go on all night: cigarette lighter flicking, beer cans popping, storming in and out of my room.

At that point in our lives, we were both filled with hate. She hated my father for what he had done to her and I hated her for drinking. I saw my father's madness in the eyes of my mother and I felt it in myself. On that particular day, as the afternoon met the evening hours, Mother's sporadic movement between the kitchen and her bedroom continued. Occasionally she walked back to my room and just stood in the doorway holding onto its frame, not saying a word, looking at me with those large, wild eyes. I would take a deep breath and hold it until she walked away. Then she would go back to the kitchen, but it was not long before she returned, making it hard for me to stay focused. Before I knew it, she was standing in the doorway again, yelling more about him—the same things over and over. She could go on and off like a light switch. Where my father had left off with the yelling, name calling and abuse, my mother picked up, reliving it everyday. It was apparent the death of my father would not be the death of his abuse. His ghost was alive, living in both of us, haunting us in death as he had in life, especially Mother, and there was no place to run to get away from his ghost.

I had gotten up several times from my desk to escort her from my room. She would stay away just long enough to smoke a cigarette and finish off a beer. The escorting became pushing as I tried to avoid her swinging arms. I knew she was trying to hit my father and not me. She was close to hysterical. As her yelling filled the house, I became frightened of her.

"Mother, I have to study. Please leave me alone," I begged her.

She staggered back and forth, looking at me with empty eyes and left the room again. I pulled the biology book back in front of me: ... *specialized tissues: xylem, which is involved in structural support and water conduction, and phloem, which functions in food conduction.*

But my plea did not last long. Before I knew it, I felt her standing behind me. Then, suddenly, there was a tug at my hair on the back of my head. As I turned in my chair, she yanked, and I felt the fist-full of hair rip from my scalp.

"I hate you!" she screamed.

"What are you doing?" I yelled, as I felt the back of my head. It stung.

Mother stood a foot from me, her fist closed tightly, clutching the patch of hair.

"I wish you were never born! I wish none of you were ever born! I should have never married that bastard. I regret the day I met him!"

"Mother! Stop it!

"I hate you! I hate you! I hate you, Woody!

I thought she was going to hit me. Like a reflex, my hand shot at her and before I was aware of what I had done, I had slapped her across the face. My mother's body stumbled back into the hallway as she felt her cheek. Her eyes were seething, like they could shoot fire. Unable to regain her footing, whether due to the large amount of alcohol she had consumed or to the force of my hand, she lost her balance. My father had become alive in me. I was no longer the little boy shaking in the corner, eyes filling with tears, watching my father beat her, watching her fall. I was now the cause of her pain.

Mother fell, landing on the bathroom floor across the small hallway. Her head rested at the base of the toilet. For a few seconds I stood over her in shock and disbelief at what I had done, terrified she was dead. I felt sick at my stomach. I could not take a breath, as my heart seemed to stop beating.

Then she moved. A slight sense of relief passed though me.

"Look what you have done to me. I hate you."

Cautiously I leaned over to help her up, hoping she would not take another swing, but at the same time feeling I deserved for her to hit me. She appeared to be okay. The most damage I had done was to her pride, but my heart was damaged forever. We stood in the hallway not saying a word. I put my arms around her and began to cry.

"It's all right," Mother said.

She rested her head on my shoulder. After a few moments I went back to my room and Mother went into her bedroom. I heard her rustle around in the bottom of her closet, then her footsteps headed toward the kitchen and a new bottle of whiskey hit against the rim of a glass.

For the next few hours, I sat at my desk listening to her going back and forth between her bedroom and the kitchen, the flickering of her cigarette lighter, and the bottle hitting the glass until the second bottle was finished. In -between one of her trips, I snuck in the kitchen while she lay in bed. I found the bottle and poured half of what was left out and replaced it with water. I went back to my room, closed my books and stacked them off to the side. I pulled out a road map of the United States from the top drawer and plotted out my trip. I-20 across Alabama. US-78 through Mississippi and Tennessee. I-40 through Oklahoma, Texas, New Mexico and Arizona. I-10 to California. Two-thousand two-hundred seventy-five miles, maybe three thousand. Three days, four at the most. Thirty -five, maybe forty hours.

I took the rest of my books and papers out of my book bag and replaced them with some clothes. I tip-toed out of the house, down the back steps, to the car. I tossed the bag on the back seat. I put the key in the ignition with the map in my lap. I sat there and looked forward.

Just go I told myself, just go. The next day she seemed to have forgotten the incident. However, I would never forget. She had called me Woody. It was the first clear episode of schizophrenia I had seen in her. For a moment she thought I was her husband and the rage burst out of her—all over me.

There truly is a fine line between love and hate. I know a part of her wished that she had never met my father. She deserved someone else who would have supported her in the pursuit of her dreams. At the same time, I knew I deserved a mother who was strong and stable, who could support me. So, there were the times that I felt I really hated her, too: when I would come home and find her drunk; during the sleepless nights when she would not stop talking about the past; the times I forced her fingers loose from around the neck of a bottle; the times I had to hold her down on the bed until she passed out to keep her from leaving the house; or the times I had to rush her to the emergency room to have her stomach pumped.

I desperately wanted to be a "normal" kid with a "normal" mother. I felt that if I was putting off my dreams of moving to California in order to go to college for her, that the least she could do was to stop drinking. But it was hard to hate her for long. We were too much alike and, no matter how hard it had gotten, I remembered how it was before. How it was sitting with her on the swing on the front porch of the farmhouse and listening to her sing. I remembered the nights she stayed up with me when I was having growing pains in my legs, and how she would rub them and tell me stories until I fell asleep. She had lots of stories to tell that I must have heard hundreds of times: stories like the one about Gene Autry; stories about how she fell in love with my father and all the boys who had tried to court her before; stories of living in France and how the Frenchmen would follow her around in the market, and how, since she was not very good at speaking French, she would hold up her ring finger and shrug her shoulders to let them know she was married. Needless to say, I never turned the ignition of the car that night. I un-packed the few clothes from my book bag and filled it back up with my college texts and papers and put the map back in the desk drawer.

Gypsies, Tramps & Thieves

Christopher graduates from college today. I am up early deciding what to wear, something to make me blend into the crowd. Dugan is attempting to run off with a shoe from the pair I just pulled out of the closet. Foolishly I yell at him to drop it. I still forget, at times, he can not hear a word. I grab him by the collar just in time before he makes it through the door into the hallway. He is getting so big and has a mind of his own. I can not help but think about my own college graduation thirty-something years ago. It was in August, too. I am having second thoughts about going as I sit down on the edge of the bed. As much as I want to be there, I feel like I may be intruding on Christopher's family time. I wonder what his sister's reaction will be if she sees me? Will she approach me and say hello? Or will she just glare at me from a distance? She knows what I look like from Christopher's myspace page. That is how she found out about us; she saw the beach pictures from a recent trip to California and Dugan's puppy pictures. I am sure it was a total shock to her system: first to find out that her younger brother is gay, and then a week later that his boyfriend is thirty years his senior. Instantly I became "the dirty old man" in her mind.

Up until then, only his father knew he was gay. Christopher came out to him about a year ago. I was in Los Angeles doing an art installation when he called wanting to know what I thought about telling his dad he was gay. Being so close to finals, I suggested he wait until the exams were over in case his father took the news badly. I was concerned that if, indeed, the news did not set well, then Christopher would be preoccupied with worry about his father's reaction and not concentrate on studying. He ended up telling him anyway. His father was shocked, but took it well. He told Christopher to hold off telling his mother or anyone else for awhile. She is very religious and it might be difficult for her to handle. Plus, she was in the middle of planning his sister's wedding coming up in a few months.

His sister was quite the investigator. One weekend when she had dropped by their parents' home when Christopher was there for the weekend with Dugan, she got my name off of Dugan's ID tag. Christopher told his parents the dog belonged to a friend, for whom he occasionally dog sat. She then googled me, finding out I was an artist and writer. And gay. Then, a week later she found Christopher's myspace page and mine, too. They had a heated discussion over the phone, more like a big disagreement. She told him he was being foolish, that I was too old for him and I was just taking advantage of his youth. It was a scenario Christopher and I had talked about before. I knew that would be everyone's first reaction. After she had had some time to cool off and digest the situation, she sent me an email of apology. I responded just to support Christopher in his decisions and left it at that.

But today I am nervous if indeed I do see her and unsure how I will feel seeing his father, older brother and mother, too. Especially his mother. I have been particularly sensitive about her because of the loss of mine and the vulnerability of our relationship over the years. I know his mother is so proud of Christopher, and I feared my presence might somehow tarnish the day for her even if she is unaware of my existence.

I get dressed despite Dugan's repeated attempts to rearrange my wardrobe. The clock by the bed shows 7:30 and I realize I need to get on the road. The University of Georgia, in Athens, is just over an hour's drive. I chase Dugan out of the bedroom and into the living room, then three or four times around the kitchen island. He knows I am trying to catch him to put him in his crate. He can not be trusted in the house running free. To Dugan, everything is a play toy, including the furniture. Once I had left him in the backyard alone where he rearranged the outdoor furniture and dragged the grill across the patio.

Fifteen minutes later I walk out the door. I sat in my black XJS in the driveway in a pair of Brooks Brothers gray flat-front slacks, a Banana Republic light blue-and-white button-down shirt and navy jacket, and the black Kenneth Cole loafers that Dugan would have loved to have eaten, and cry; respectfully dressed up with somewhere to go, but I can not bring myself to turn the key in the ignition.

After ten minutes or so, I wipe my eyes and go back

inside. I then change clothes and take Dugan for a walk in
Piedmont Park just a few blocks from the house. I know
the graduation ceremonies are scheduled to start at 9:30. I
wait until then and send Christopher a text message: Congratulations! I love you! Moments later, I receive one
back from him: Where r u sitting? I sit down on a bench
near a group of dogwood trees, staring at the message,
wondering how I should respond, as Dugan gets tangled
up in the leash. I wonder if Christopher is looking in the
crowd for his mother, as I had done at my graduation for
mine. He is her golden boy as I was mine. And I wonder if
he is looking for me, too? Will I disappoint him like my
mother did me?

It was time to go, or at least get a running start on a
departure long overdue. Three years to be exact. But I
could not run. I had to take baby steps. I was too much
like her—like my mother, and I could not just leave her
behind. But, in a way, I did that very thing.
I had finished college in three years by going the summer quarters. I knew at the beginning I could not stop, not
even for a break, until I had that diploma in my hand. I
lived at home with her while attending Mercer University
in Macon, Georgia—a twenty- minute car ride north. I had
never really intended on going to college; besides, while
my father was alive he had told me he could not afford to
send me. It was just as well. I had a dream—a big one—
but it was interrupted. My mother found out about the GI
Bill signed into law on June 22, 1944, by President Roose-
velt. It would pay for my college tuition because I was a
dependent of a deceased war veteran. She insisted I go to
college because she had always wanted to herself, but her
family had been too poor to send her when she was my

age. "A college education is something they can never take away from you, Son," she said. So, I went for her. I would wait to move to California until after I finished.

Three years later, as planned, I had finally made it to graduation day. The chapel bells chimed, signaling the beginning of the ceremonies. As families and friends moved into the church to take their seats for the auspicious day, the excitement carried from the gardens into the chapel. The graduating class of the summer of nineteen–hundred-and- seventy-seven lined up for the long awaited moment. We started up the chapel stairs one by one, the large red doors opened wide for us. I looked up into the sky. The position of the sun was right over the chapel, and from my angle it looked like it was being pierced by the sharp point of the steeple. As I entered I could see the rows of people standing, looking back as the graduates filed in. I looked over my shoulder to see any sign of Mother and my sister. Perhaps I had missed them in the gardens and they had already taken their seats; I hoped.

Seconds later, music filled the chapel from the pipe organ as the President of the University took his place at the podium. He gave a congratulatory speech commending everyone's hard work and achievements, and giving encouragement for our bright futures. As the names were called, the audience cheered and applauded each graduate's achievement. Then, my name rang out. I stood up and walked to the stage, looking into the rows of people again, looking for my mother and sister; my ears waiting to hear their cheers. There were some random acknowledgements, but not from them. They had not come. An hour later, it was over. The graduates stood, tossing their caps high into the air as the chapel filled again with waves of more roars of cheers and applause. I held my cap to my side as the celebration spilled out into the garden. I skirted the perimeter of the crowd, dashing across the lawn. The shadow of the chapel covered me as I ran toward the steps leading down to the street. As I stopped for a moment at the top to catch my breath, my eyes caught a figure of a woman below. She was staggering, trying to master the steep climb, holding on to the railing. With closer observation, I saw my sister's car, below on the street, as it sped off out of sight.

"Mother, what are you doing?" I questioned. "Be careful! Where's Sandra going?"

"She's mad at me," Mother slurred. "We had a fight. Has the graduation started yet?"

I approached her on the stairs, reaching for her arm. She looked up at me.

"Let's go," I urged, guiding her back down.

Once we reached the bottom, I handed her my diploma. She clutched it to her breasts.

"I missed it?"

I could see the tears fill her eyes. My heart began to break.

"It's okay. The important thing is you're here now."

"You did it, Son. You're the first in our family to graduate from college," she said, as her tears gently fell on the diploma, each one representing a lost aspiration.

I wiped her cheeks with the sleeve of my gown.

"No, Mother, you did it. It's your diploma, your graduation. I want you to keep it. Congratulations. I love you," I said, wishing she had a better life, truly longing for her the happiness she had been unable to obtain. I hoped the diploma would give her some optimism for her future.

I continued to sit on the park bench, hoping Christopher was enjoying his big day with his family; wondering if he realized his accomplishments, graduating as student of the year in his department and Cum Laude. Dugan had managed to untangle himself. He began playing tug-of-war with the leg of my jeans as my mind relived my big day. Then, unfortunately, I did not feel a sense of accomplishment, but rather disappointment. Everything that I had imagined that would be different was not. Three years later and my graduation had not changed anything in our lives during that time. My mother continued to struggle with the past, unable to divorce it as I had hoped, and I found myself more afraid of the future than ever before. I felt alone—not only for myself, but for her as well. I can not go to California now, with her in such a state, I thought to myself as she held on tightly to my arm. Who will look after her if I go? It was clear that Steven and Sandra had gone their own ways; trying to make a life for themselves out of the wreckage our father had left behind. The sadness in my mother's eyes, on my graduation day, stared back at me as we walked to the car. It was added reason for her to drink on such a day.

After graduation, it was apparently clear I could not leave my mother behind. I took out a student loan to start a master's program in education at Mercer. But I had to take the first baby step out of Warner Robins. I moved to Macon. Although my heart was still set on California, it would have to wait a little longer. I had already left Shoney's, the job my brother had gotten me a few years back when he called one Mother's Day telling me they needed help making strawberry pies. After that, I began flipping hamburgers and making more pies until my last year of college, when I got a job in the Men's Department of Macy's at the Macon Mall.

The night before I moved out, I had a conversation with my mother as I sat next to her at the table. I could tell she was trying to be strong, but her sorrowful and droopy eyes were telling.

"Son, I know you need to be on your own. It's time."

"Are you going to be okay? I'm just twenty, thirty minutes max away."

"I'll be fine. Don't worry yourself."

She moved her hand from the cup of coffee and placed it on top of mine.

"You know you're my heart, Son. Right?"

"Yes, Mother, as you're mine."

"Well then. I'll be okay if you're okay."

Then she squeezed my fingers as hard as she could. As hard as she loved me.

"Ouch. What a grip you have."

"That's how much I love you, Son. That's how much I love all my children."

My mother released her grip, returning her hand to the cup. She took another sip and then reached for the lit cigarette smoldering in the ashtray. She took a yawning drag, held it for a few seconds before exhaling the smoke back into the already saturated air.

"You go on to bed now, Son. I'm going to sit here for awhile."

I stood up.

"I'll be okay," she reminded me before taking in another drag of smoke.

"Mother, those things are going to kill you one day. When are you going to stop smoking?"

"I'm working on it. One day I'll give them up, besides, I don't really inhale them."

"Right," I said sarcastically.

I leaned down to kiss her on the cheek.

"Okay," I said.

"Remember, I'll be okay if you're okay, Son."

I walked through the opening between the breakfast room and the kitchen, just steps away from the living room we seldom entered after my father's death. I stopped in my tracks for a second, turning my head to look at her sitting alone under the light that accentuated the loneness inside of her, and the consuming night that surrounded her even in daylight. She sat there well into the deepest part of that night. The wall of jalousie windows were rolled opened. A number of the textured glass slats were missing, but it was hard to tell while they were fully extended saturating the house with the color of night. The blackness collided with the harsh light from the dish-shaped fixture over the table. Below, the ashtray was overflowing with nervously stubbed-out butts as my mother sipped on a tepid cup of coffee from the day-old pot on the stove. Her profile was submerged in the hazy cigarette-smoke-filled room, strong with the smells of tobacco, coffee and trepidation.

On that last night in the house, I sat for hours on my bed and cried—the bed I had run to from my father's belt—afraid of what I would find "out there" and worrying about my mother, wondering if I were doing the right thing by moving, feeling I was deserting her, leaving her alone with my father's ghost. I knew she did not want me to go, but she knew I had to. I stared at the walls and ceiling of my room in fear of what my mother's life would be like after I moved. But I still had to go, fully believing it would not be that much dissimilar from when I lived in the house with her. I just hoped it would not be worse. I knew she was happy for me, but unable to show it. Any happiness she had was trapped under all her pain and misery. I feared the loneliness she would have to deal with in an empty house. And my biggest concern: my father. He would still be there, even in death. The pain of her life would be closer after I was gone and the ghost of her husband more prevalent. My departure meant I was leaving her alone with him. For the past three years it had just been the three of us in the house: my mother, my father's ghost and I.

I had wanted the outcome to be different, so different than the reality she was living; the one we both were. I had mistakenly thought she would have a better life after his death. I had prayed for it—for a change for the better and for the faded light in her to spark up again so she could finally begin to live her life as she was meant to. The life interrupted by my father. Yes, I knew she was afraid. We were both afraid for her.

After his death, I had wanted my mother to sell the house, to pack up her belongings and get out, and perhaps the real hell she was living would become a distant memory of the past. The house was too much of a reminder of him. The walls had absorbed his smell, his anger, and the echo of the fatal shot that rang throughout the house, puncturing not only his flesh but all our souls as my father had lain on the sofa in the living room and pulled the trigger of the rifle he had placed in his mouth. His blood exploded not only into the air, into the smallest crevices of the walls, and into the densest fibers of the sofa and carpet, but into the deepest parts of ourselves as well. I should have burned the house down. Call it survival or fear or selfishness, I had to leave. It was not an easy decision, and there were many behind my departure. To minimize my guilt, I held on tightly to the knowledge that

throughout history sons leave their mothers; it was un-
natural for a son to stay, no matter how much alike we
were.

I had intended on leaving much sooner than I did, and
had planned to put a great distance between me and Warner Robins, not just the twenty miles or so between it and
Macon. From the age of sixteen, two years before my father's demise, I had always believed I belonged in Los
Angeles, California. Upon graduation from high school, I
thought I would finally begin a journey that would take
me far from the misery that had been a part of me almost
from birth. The dream of leaving was the only thing that
kept me sane, and perhaps alive. An eccentric kind of excitement had begun to grow inside me over the summer
that preceded my senior year. But then the summer heat
began to wane, the faint smells of Fall began to fill the air,
and the echo from the firing of a rifle filled the house on
the east end of Shirley Drive. With the pull of a trigger,
my plans and my dreams were delayed.

Why and how I came to the decision to move to California might seem bizarre to many, but it was a place that
seemed to be made of dreams and the farthest I could get
away from Georgia without leaving the continent. And,
perhaps, it could be everything "home" was not. It all began with the *Sonny & Cher Show*, and then just *Cher*—
after their highly publicized split—that I began to think
the west coast was "the place for me," and not *Green
Acres,* another show where poor Eva Gabor was stuck in
Hooterville in the middle of nowhere as I was in Warner
Robins. This realization-of-sorts came to me all of a sudden while watching Cher—the diva—sing one of her solos
dressed "to the nines" in a Bob Mackie gown. Being so
taken by the dresses, I should have suspected that I was

gay, though, at the time, I thought I had a crush on Cher; instead it was the glittery sequins! Every Sunday night, without fail, I sat in front of the old fossil of a television made to look like a piece of brown Mediterranean furniture, and held my breath until a few lines into the song, in a radically spectacular way, she stripped off her outer gown and revealed lots of skin as she licked her lips and flipped her long, black hair over her shoulders, one side at a time.

The television screen was usually fuzzy, despite the rabbit ears twisted and turned in every possible direction, but that small difficulty did not stop me from watching. If, by chance, I was lucky enough to be alone in the house, I covered my head in a well-worn bath towel and licked my lips and flipped my towel-hair right along with her. And, if I was not alone, I went to the bathroom and did a bit of lip licking and towel-hair flicking while mouthing *Gypsies, Tramps & Thieves* post show in the mirror. I can honestly say it was the only real drag I have ever done but, after just one season, I became a pro at the lip licking and hair-flicking. It goes without saying that, as a teenager, I was in love with Cher, and California was the place I had to be!

Cher was something to look forward to all week, and I tingled with excitement when Friday came, knowing that she would be visiting my living room in just two more days. For an hour I was able to escape the reality of my life and the loneliness that filled my days. There was nothing for a boy like me to do in the small, repressed Air Force and football town. It was even worse during the long, scorching summers when the show was on hiatus. All a young boy could do was dream about her lengthy fake eyelashes, shiny waist-length black hair, flowing beaded gowns and wait for the new Fall season to begin. Then, as another season and Sunday night finally arrived, I sat cross-legged on the floor inches from the screen, my heart sinking a little each time I noticed the hour was getting shorter. Before I knew it, there was Sonny standing next to Cher as they said their goodbyes and began singing, "*I Got You, Babe.*" So, I was left broken hearted, waiting another whole week to see her again. Then, my depression would set in as she said her good-nights to her number one devoted fan—me—and licked her lips and flicked her hair a few more times. The show was over and I went to bed dreaming of California.

I had to go; not to ride the big surf, or to become a movie star, but because that was where Cher lived. Somehow I seemed to think I could relate to her not having ever met except on the television screen; I believed we were sort of soul mates. Cher was different, and so was I. She had struggled and so had I. Cher was a gypsy, a rebel, and I was feeling like one more and more as I came to face a dark truth.

Secrets Out in the Open

"I'm not gay!" I adamantly avowed.

"It's, it's okay if you are," my mother hesitated. "I still love you."

Despite her declaration, it was very clear she hated the idea of having a gay son by the stressed look on her face and by her uncomfortable posture in the doorway.

"What makes you think that?"

"Your sister and I were talking about it on the phone. I told her you were modeling in Atlanta."

"Really? And what does gay have to do with that?"

"Well," Mother paused her thought.

"Well, what?"

"She said most men who do that kind of thing are gay."

"Well, she's mistaken! I'm not gay!"

I had decided to never tell my mother; I feared it

would be another huge disappointment in her life of disappointments. I could just hear her, in the back of my head, asking me what she had done wrong to make me that way. I was completely convinced she would blame herself for me wanting to be with a man. She was just that way—everything was her fault: her abusive marriage; her husband's suicide; her oldest son's bad grades and dropping out of high school; her daughter's periods of rebellion and dropping out of college to join the Army; the estrangement of her children in general; her younger son being a homosexual. No! I could not do that to her. The truth would eat at her like all the disappointments and failures in her life had, and I could not add another one to the list. I could not let her take the blame for having a gay son, too! Two men together was something I believed she could not ever understand. If I could prevent it, I was never going to allow her to carry another burden on a back that was already overloaded with grief and heartbreak. Plus, I myself was very uncomfortable with the idea of being gay, and I would rather not deal with it or discuss it, especially with my mother.

In the face of that fear, I did come close to telling her the night before I moved to Macon while we sat at the kitchen table. I thought about telling her then, at that very moment when she was squeezing the blood out of my finger tips until they hurt. I opened my mouth. The muscles around my lips began to form the three words I felt I needed to tell her—I am gay. But then my mouth closed, and after that night I did my best to keep my secret from her.

Because of that secret, I knew I had to leave, especially if I could not tell her the one scary truth I was finding out about my self. The truth I had suppressed and the main reason I had to go: I would not be able to survive in a small town. I was also afraid of being like the effeminate gay twins in their thirties who lived up the street with their mother, they were the subject of gossip and ridicule. I could not be a mommy's boy and gay, too. Living in Warner Robins made me feel like I was suffocating; asphyxiating on the toxic smells of a troubled past and an uncertain future. Even before my father killed himself, I had felt like a dog kept on a chain; confined to a small circular world, the center of it being a large oak tree. My "oak tree" was Warner Robins, Georgia. I wanted to break the chain and run free. I wanted to get as far away as possible and live the mammoth dreams that only a sad little boy can imagine in the loneliest parts of his soul, shut up in his room from the rest of the world. Much like my mother had, at my age, amassed lots of dreams for herself: to get as far away from the cotton, the farm, and Fayette, Alabama—her own oak tree. I needed her to understand my dreams as I understood hers.

I was good at keeping secrets. I never told her about the neighbor man, whose grass I use to cut. He would stand in the windows of his house, watching me with his hands in his over-sized boxer shorts while playing with himself. Or of how he once took me off in his car and tried to sexually assault me, but I opened the car door and ran. Later on, I found out that Sandra was keeping secrets, too, about how our father abused her for years. I had my own deeply hidden thoughts and concerns about my father as well, that I was too afraid to face—even today. He always made me hang out with him, doing yard work, insisting I take off my shirt as his eyes stared at my flesh, his hands touching me. Later the nightmares came with the screams in my sleep, as my mother ran to my room to calm me down. Secrets too deep, scarred-over and buried by years of disbelief, fear and apprehensions. Years later, Mother found out about my father well after his suicide. Another crushing burden for her to have to live with.

At one point, early-on, I thought my homosexual feelings were a result of the bad and twisted relationship I had had with my father, and perhaps my mother's weaknesses: booze, insecurity, and low self-esteem might have played a part. Up until then, I had convinced myself that any crushes I had had on men previously were because of that low esteem and that I just wanted to be more like them, that I was not really gay. I never really considered the fact that I might have been born that way. I was confused. I liked girls, in fact, had some huge crushes, so it is beyond me why I turned out gay, but there was another part of me that thought more and more about men, and the need to be comforted by the same sex. I just kept hoping I would meet the "right girl" to end those unwanted desires. And, trust me, I tried. There had been a number of girls—pretty girls—in my young life. Two in high school and several while in college and after; and I had thought my mother would never have reason to wonder about my sexual identity, or even entertain the notion that she had a gay son.

There was Mary Ann, my sophomore year of high school. Her pretty blue eyes and long blonde hair, down to her waist, fueled the fantasies of boys on the edge of puberty. I followed her around for a week, with my shiny, new ID bracelet in my pocket, getting up the nerve to ask her to be my girlfriend. I ended up slipping it into her coat pocket on a Friday while I walked her home after school. She had it on the following Monday. I was crushed when her father moved the family to Cairo, Georgia. Then, in my senior year, there was Laura, from a very prominent family. She ended up becoming a Breck Shampoo model. The summer before college there was Katie, a dark-haired and dark-eyed waitress at Shoney's who was going to the local technical school. We got caught in an innocent kiss in the breakfast room one afternoon by Mother.

"My baby's growing into a man. I like her. She's a pretty girl," Mother blushed, as she told me after Katie left.

Then there was Susan, an older divorced woman in my art history class. She had been the wife of a powerful Macon attorney. After a messy divorce, she decided to go back to college. The first day I saw her she looked like she had stepped out of an issue of *Vogue*. We had lunch a few times at the pizza place just off campus. One night I ended up in her bathtub, full of bubbles, drinking wine. But the evening was cut short after I had called my mother to check in and let her know I would be home late. She was drunk and distressed, so I drove back to Warner Robins and to my mother.

With college behind me and California and Cher on hold again, I rented a small, corner efficiency apartment in the Massey building in Macon not far from the campus. Finally, I was out of my dead father's house. I continued to reassure my mother that I was only a phone call away and less than thirty minutes by car, but the first week in my new place I stayed only two nights; the rest I spent back home. On the nights I did stay in my apartment, I called my mother every few hours to check on her.

My first apartment was on the second floor overlooking College Street, which was lined with big, old southern mansions. Ironically, it was several blocks up from one of the private mental facilities where my mother had been a patient shortly after we moved from Columbus, Georgia to Warner Robins when I was a child. Again, my brother, sister and I sat in the car waiting for our father to return from a visit. And I can remember looking out the window imagining what it would be like living in one of the stately homes.

The Massey's beautiful brick exterior was majestic with large glass and ornate iron arched doors leading into a polished black-and-white tiled lobby floor. My apartment had one large room with hardwood floors, a small kitchen off to the side, a closet-sized bathroom, and the best feature: bright white French doors leading to a small wrought iron balcony with a view of the garages and the parking lot.

I met Betsy, and later, Monica shortly after starting at Macy's. They were both art majors. Betsy took my virginity. She had graduated from Wesleyan College. Monica was two years behind her. They were both pretty, but very different. Betsy, the "older woman," was fair-skinned, tall, slender and very fashionable, with short brown hair cut high on her neck while falling longer on the sides of her face. Her light blue eyes were mischievous. On the flip side, Monica was shorter, with dark, shoulder-length hair and shadowy exotic eyes. Then I met Dennis, a school teacher, who lived on the top floor of the Massey Apartments, and I explored those deeply guarded feelings I had tried so hard to suppress.

A year later, I put my graduate studies on hold and moved to Little Five Points in Atlanta. I found Macon to be just as small and suffocating as Warner Robins, and acting on my deep desires left me distressed and anxious. I chose to move north, to a much bigger city to hide the truth, but one still close to home for my mother's sake. Atlanta was only an hour-and-a-half drive. It was not Los

Angeles, but at least I felt I was heading in the right direction; somewhat. I transferred to a Macy's there and, because of my art degree, I landed a job in visual merchandising. The fact that it was a very "gay" field of work did not help my cover-up. I told myself and everyone else I was just doing something artsy until I had my first art show and could make it on my own as an artist. Everyone in my department was gay, but I protested I was straight. I had gotten really good at keeping secrets, just like my mother. We both had had a lot of practice since childhood.

One day a photographer approached me while I was dressing mannequins in the men's suit department. He inquired if I had ever thought about modeling. I asked him if he meant "modeling" like *Gentlemen's Quarterly* modeling or that "other kind." He said the legitimate kind. At first I thought it was a "come on" line, but he was persistent. He handed me his card and told me to give him a call. The card ended up in my back pocket and eventually forgotten after it was washed in the oversized machine at the laundromat that smelled like bleach down the street from my apartment. Several weeks later, the photographer was back in the store looking for me, where he convinced me to do some test shots. I was taken by surprise when they turned out much better than I had expected. I looked like a completely different person in print. I did not appear to be the nervous, insecure, self-loathing person I was on the inside. "Perhaps I can do this," I told myself, as I remembered what two of the older ladies working in the credit department would always tell me: you should be on a soap opera. Within a few months, the photographer had set me up with a friend who worked at an agency and I was being sent out on "go sees." It was not long before I got booked on my first job and others followed shortly after, mostly fashion print ads.

I made the mistake of telling my mother about the modeling when I was home one weekend and gave her a few copies of some photos I had done for an ad.

"They're wonderful, Son. Professionally done? What did they cost?" she asked.

"There're from a job I did at a hotel."

"A job?"

"Yes, a modeling job."

I thought it would make her happy to have some nice photographs of me that she could show to her friends at church. On Sundays, before and after the church service, Mother wanted to introduce me to everyone. And I mean everyone.

"Oh, there's Gabby Littlefield. I want you to meet her."

"Do I have to?"

"Oh, come on. I'm proud of my beautiful son. Humor me. It'll make me happy. Will you?"

So, every weekend trip home, I would meet Gabby Littlefield, Doris Clements, Lisa Redwood, Joe Dixon and anyone new. It was my own fault. I had talked Mother into joining a church after I moved to Atlanta. I wanted her to meet people, particularly a man. Things had gone by the wayside with Eddie; they had lost touch months later when she broke down again and went into the hospital not long after he was sent off to Turkey.

As a family, we had never gone to church. Mother sent us to Sunday school when we lived in Germany. My sister and I joined a Methodist Church a few years before our father killed himself, but even though Mother had very strong religious convictions, she never would go with us. I was looking for some hope, something to believe in, and with the encouragement of a concerned neighbor and member of the church who seemed to understand what was going on within my family, I set out to find religion and God. At night for years from a child's bed, I prayed to Him to shield us from my father's violence, to save my mother from her insanity, to save us all. I sat in the pews, holding my Bible tightly in my hands looking for peace and security. So, I was surprised when Mother agreed to go with me when I was home. She just wanted to be with me; my weekend trips home were the highlight of her week. By then, my sister had dropped out of college to join the Army and my brother just never came around much to see her. I wanted her to join the same church Sandra and I had. It had a large congregation with lots of choices of available men. I was pleasantly surprised when she started going to Wednesday evening services and even on Sundays if I missed a weekend trip home. Unfortunately, she ended up joining a small Baptist Church with a very small congregation with few prospects for a new husband. And another reason to keep my secret to myself.

So, we sat in church together, I playing the role of the devoted, straight son and my mother pretending to be happy and content. She hid her past, the amount of liquor she had consumed the week before, and pretended that her only mental disorder was occasional bouts of depression. Around my mother I continued to put on the façade that I was straight and made it a point to bring up girls in our conversations even after I had started going to gay bars in Atlanta. I felt extremely uncomfortable in them, but I made myself go anyway. I was ashamed, lonely, and felt—as I always did—like an outsider. My move to Atlanta had been overwhelming and it was compounded by the constant worrying about my mother's drinking and mental wellbeing back home. The dark bars of Atlanta offered a hiding place for me and my shame. My mother chose the darkness of her house. I would come home on the weekends and find her in any number of states: sober, drunk, or somewhere in-between, happy or deeply in despair, but she would try to pull it together to go to church. When I tried to talk about her drinking, she would get mad and tell me she could stop anytime she wanted. The alcohol was all she had to dull the pain inside of her and to forget about the past at least for a little while.

I needed to forget about the past as well. I needed to forget that I hated myself and felt worthless. It was years before I realized my negative feelings were a byproduct of my childhood. Until that consciousness came, I went to the bars more and more often and discovered a whole new world, very different than the one I came from. The more I realized I was gay, the harder I tried to keep it from my mother, to keep from adding to her misery and shame. I started drinking, first to get the courage up to walk into a gay bar, then I needed another to get the nerve up to carry on a conversation with a stranger. I was getting noticed, both in the bars and with the modeling. I started making friends and then the lies came out of my mouth to cover up my past and keep it hidden. A few drinks turned into more. There were mornings I could not remember how I got home; empty mornings, where I felt hollow on the inside and saw the face of my mother in the mirror. I was drinking to forget the life I came from, just like my mother. I saw myself as a hypocrite. By the time I was in my late twenties, I had several sexual encounters and was using alcohol as a crutch—like my mother.

As the years progressed, there were times I wanted to tell her, mostly to share my struggles and heartaches with the men I had dated. Like my mother, I wanted a prince to make everything okay, but there were no men on white horses. While I was looking for love, everyone else seemed to be just looking for sex. One evening, during a phone conversation with Mother, I did slip. We had both been drinking. I was upset over a guy I had been seeing for six months or so. I had just learned he had cheated on me and my mother was telling me about a man she had met.

Mother started bagging groceries for tips at the Commissary on Robins Air Force Base. She hit it off with another one of the baggers who became her dear friend, Siggy. She had carried Mother's bags out to the taxi on several occasions. Siggy told Mother they had a few openings and encouraged her to check it out. Most of the baggers were dependents or retired military. Even with bad knees, she was able to make a hundred dollars or so a week, which helped supplement her annuity and got her out of the house and around people. She had been fired from the doughnut shop years earlier for coming to work with liquor on her breath.

"This retired Captain was flirting with me today while I was bagging up his groceries. It's the second time he has asked me to bag and carry for him," Mother said.

"Really? I would say he's attracted to you."

"Yes, really! He gave me a ten-dollar tip for five bags and he had a nice car, too."

"Speaking of cars, are you ever going to learn to drive?"

"I'm too nervous."

"Mother, you can't keep walking everywhere, especially with the arthritis getting so bad in your knees. You already have a limp."

"Walking is good for them. The doctor says I need to walk. Besides, Siggy picks me up for work and there are other people I can call to take me places. And there's always Frank at the taxi company."

"Well, I would feel better if you would try harder to learn how to drive. I can take you back over to the high school parking lot and let you practice some more. You did well the last few times."

"We'll see, but what should I do when this man comes back to the commissary?"

"See what happens. Invite him over for coffee."

"That's a bad idea. You know men just have one thing on their minds."

"Yeah, you're right, especially if he's anything like Mark," I blurted out.

"Mark? Who's Mark?"

"Ah. No one. Did I say Mark?"

I took another gulp of wine.

After I realized what I had said, I quickly backpedaled.

"Uh. Uh, I was just thinking about one of the gay guys at work. He was talking about almost the same thing. I guess he's having boyfriend problems."

My mother was totally silent on the other end. "Shit," I thought to myself. "I've got to be more careful. I've got to continue hiding the truth behind the façade."

There were several occasions when I thought that it might bring us closer if I told her the truth. She might understand me better. There were so many things I wanted to tell her, things I really needed to share, but the long pause on the phone made me realize again I needed to keep the gay thing to myself. Then I thought, maybe she already knows and just does not want to deal with it.

So here we were keeping secrets from each other, totally in denial but perhaps knowing the truth about the other all along.

Then a year later, my phone rang.

"I walked out of Sunday school today!" Mother told me.

"Walked out?"

"Yes, I walked out!"

"Is something wrong?"

"Janice Moore was teaching the class. We were having a discussion on issues in the community and what involvement the church should take."

"I see. Did something upset you?"

"Yes! She was talking about homosexuals. How they are sinners. That they were all going to hell."

"It's a controversial topic, for sure. Why did that come up?"

"There's a gay bar in Macon and it got raided last week."

"Really. Interesting."

"Did you know there was a gay bar in Macon? It's apparently downtown near the college campus."

"Ah. No, not really," I lied. I had never been to it, but I knew about it.

"Well, anyway, I told them God loves everyone and Janice butted in and said that He didn't love gay people."

"Then what happened?"

"I collected my things and walked out."

"Just like that?"

"Yes. There's nothing wrong with someone being gay."

"You really think that?"

"Yes. Some people are just born that way."

Christmas Lights

Time has collected quickly, filling Mother's box of memories with bits and pieces almost to the top. As I dig toward the bottom, many reminders of "how we were," like pointing fingers, jab at my heart; while tightly clenched fists punch me relentlessly in the stomach. It is all there—a lifetime in the form of every little trinket or anything representative of a moment or event that needed to be remembered and cherished in the future. She kept everything. Every card, letter, note, token, even her gift cards from the wedding presents she received sixty years ago. The dining room table, the chairs and floor are covered with boxes and boxes filled with nostalgia; overflowing with keepsakes—every memory, modest to titanic, that she held dear to her heart. There are photographs, too, filling more boxes. There are hands full of rolls of unde-

215

veloped film in an old shoe box that have been lying quietly over the decades waiting to be processed. They all
represent my mother's life: the silly little handmade crafts
I made in grade school; young years of construction-paper
red hearts trimmed in white lace—now grayed—for Val-
entines Day; a necklace I made for her in the fifth-grade
out of cheap, gaudy, multicolored plastic beads—which
she had worn as proudly as if it had been made of rare dia-
monds. Among the collection, a jewelry box, with a green
felt lining, made from covering the outside of a cigar box
with seashells—some now missing, others rattling in the
bottom of the box in which it was found. There are crayon
drawings on craft paper created by all three of her children; the lopsided mug I made in the third grade; Steven's
ribbons from sporting endeavors; Sandra's hair barrettes
and her first baby shoes; and our report cards with jotted
notes from teachers on progress and failures from kinder-
garten through high school. On one, Mrs. Ringer wrote:
*Randy has adjusted well to his class, but lacks skill in col-
oring.* Mrs. Landis, my first grade teacher: *Randy is making definite strides in maturing and I feel summer school
will also benefit him in this area. He needs constant study
and practice in all areas of work, and gaining self-
confidence.* Mrs. McDonald, my second grade teacher:
*Randy's reading skills are still a problem, however he
tries. He needs more help in spelling.* Even today, I continue to struggle with these challenges.

There are the stacks of cards and letters I sent to her,
among others from my sister, with foreign postage, a few
from our brother, all bound separately by cracked rubber
bands and pieces of aged ribbon. They were tucked away
in messy drawers, and in old dusty, ragged boxes stacked
in a closet of the house—twenty-five years of trying to

reach out to her. While years tend to fade reality, the content of those drawers and boxes—back in the custody of the hands from which they were first created—sharpens it once again. Where time has dimmed the harsh memories, seeing the brittle pages covered with faded ink turn up the light until I am blinded by an array of emotions: sorrow and heartache, longing, and even comfort. Yes, comfort! These pages bring back a flood of recollections, and my mind flashes like I am sitting in a movie theater watching my own life and, more importantly, my mother's. All my senses are jolted. I suddenly remember the faint smells of childhood mixed together in the bowl of life: freshly cut grass, chlorine from the public pool, the booze-laden breath of my father, blown-out birthday candles, the smell of a new puppy, cookies and cakes baking in a hot oven, and my mother's Chanel No. 5 perfume. Then come the reminders of the changing of the seasons and what they bring: the yearning hopes that bloom in Spring, the feel of Summer's persistent heat on my skin and its fire stinging the lining of my nostrils, the soporific quiet of the Fall days where you can almost hear the leaves break away from the tree limbs, and the diminutive, icy-cold days of winter and the solitude they bring.

There is one letter—tightly held in my fingers' grip—which I keep reading over and over.

Dear Mother,

I am sorry our visits have not been very good. The next time I come I will take you to lunch if you would like.

Please try to understand your children only want what is best for you. You will not get any better until you stop thinking that everyone is against you. We love you. We all have our lives to live and it is time you started liv-

ing yours. You have a lot ahead of you. You do have a future.

We want to help you, but you have to start helping yourself first. Put the past behind you and look to the future.

I love you,
Randy

It is good advice: Put the past behind and look to the future. Good advice even I did not take to heart for myself.

It is the Christmas cards that get to me the most. All the Christmas mornings flood my head as far back as I can remember. There was always a tree and the presents my parents could not really afford. The early holidays were happy, where the later ones were a façade and weak ones at that. They could not cover up the truth of our lives, and especially my mother's.

I am holding a card dated 1983 with an angel on the front and a few remaining sparkles of glitter. I had been in Atlanta for two years. On the inside I wrote:

Looking forward to seeing you for Christmas.
Love you,
Randy.

It is Christmas morning. Early. Too early to wake up and be alone. From my bed I can see the stack of presents for my mother on the table in the long hallway. I must admit they are wrapped to perfection: A bottle of Chanel No. 5—a must—a simple, but lovely print dress I found on sale at Neiman Marcus and several other little things I got at Macy's with my twenty-percent employee discount. I hope they will make her happy, I think, as I lie in bed. After all, it is just another day to me, but for her it is about making her happy; trying to make up for all the misery in her life that I am realizing, no matter how hard or much I wish, she will never be able to escape, because that misery is a part of her like an organ the body must have to stay alive. But I continue to hope and wish anyway, and sometimes pray.

I wrap my head in a pillow, feeling like I have a bit of a hangover from the night before. My head hurts a little. The bar was crowded; most gay bars usually are on Christmas Eve. Either you are getting that one last night out before you have to face the family the next day, or you have recently arrived into town and, after spending a few hours with your relatives, you realize you have to go someplace you feel comfortable—quickly—before you explode into a million pieces, like a fruit cake, all over the Christmas tree. I hate Christmas and holidays in general where family is involved. Wait—they are all about family. Yes, I hate them all. I know today will be hard on both of us, and I wonder what condition I will find Mother in when I get home. I hope it will not be like last year, or the year before, or the year before.

It is a double whammy for me. Not only do I hate Christmas, but I hate gay bars as well. I am not feeling so great about myself for staying in town on Christmas Eve instead of driving down to Warner Robins. I should have driven home last night. I should not have left my mother alone on such an important night. Besides the hangover, Christmas morning greets me with guilt in my belly. Why I continue to go to the bars is beyond me. I guess I am hoping to find my prince charming; hoping he is waiting for me like a Christmas present. After all, meeting someone special is up there with miracles, and what better time to find a miracle than Christmas Eve. Hope is such a double-sided-sword; I end up getting stabbed either way.

I almost brought someone home last night. I am relieved I refrained from letting my loneliness and hormones get the best of me. Richard, I think, was his name, living in Miami. His parents live in Buckhead, off West Paces Ferry Road close to the Governor's Mansion, he told me. I wanted to gag, but he was hot. Perhaps if he still lived in town I might have taken him home. Luckily for me, I am twenty-eight-years old and have smartened-up. There would be no point in bringing this Richard home regardless of how hot he was. I already knew the scenario the second he told me he was from out of town. Of course, most of the men in the bar last night were from out of town. It would just be a roll in the bed and he would be on his way back to his parents' fabulous Buckhead manor before the engine of his mother's Mercedes cooled down. Besides, I had clean sheets on the bed and it would have meant another trip down to the laundry room.

Finally out of bed, I showered the bar smoke off my skin, groomed and dressed. I want to look good for my mother. I want to make her proud; if I look good for her today, then I know she will feel good about herself if only for a short time. She has asked me so many times: how did I produce such a beautiful child? Of course all mothers think their children are beautiful. I always took it as a compliment even though I never saw it. But my mother is the one that is beautiful. Truly! And I know she fears she has lost it before she had the chance to live her life; before she can accomplish her dream—to be a beautiful woman on stage singing, with everyone in the audience admiring her voice and her beauty.

Christmas Lights

I load up the presents in my arms and walk out the door to the car, wondering again, how I will find her when I get home. We talked on the phone last night, before I went out to the bar, which, of course, I did not tell her I was heading. I told her I was too tired to drive, that I would come first thing in the morning. I had not come out to her yet, still afraid she would be disappointed in me. After all, I was the one she was looking toward to make it, to become successful. She sounded fine, but I could tell she already had a few holiday drinks in her.

In just under two hours I am back in Warner Robins. Even though it is only ninety-eight miles, it seems like a million. God, how I hate this town. Every time I come back, I am amazed how I survived it.

I have been driving under a light rain most of the trip. I would rather it be snowing. That way, it would feel more like Christmas—like in all the movies. It is not even cold, more like an overcast Fall day. The road is wet. The windshield wipers are set on delay. I watch the droplets listlessly collect on the glass. First a few, then they multiply more and more until my vision is slightly distorted. Then the wipers squeegee them away just before I lose sight of the roadway, and the cycle starts all over again like a clean slate. I wish my mother could wipe her slate clean and start all over again, I think to myself.

The traffic on the highway is light and even lighter once I get into town. The main drag, Watson Boulevard, is empty. The telephone poles lining both sides of the street are adorned with an array of lighted holiday decorations that appear to be made out of colored, shiny garland: gold, silver, red, and green. They are large, in silhouette, and look flimsy: a bell, a round ornament, a present with a bow, and a star. One after the other my car rushes by them at forty-five miles an hour. I turn down Lumpkin Street for a short distance, pass the cemetery where I notice more decorations on the headstones: more shiny, colored garland; small, plastic Christmas trees; and potted poinsettias. There are a few people standing over the graves. Seeing them makes me sadder. I turn on Shirley Drive. I pass Euclid Circle where our old house is at the end of the cul-de-sac, and in a few more blocks I pull into the driveway. The ivy has taken over the four tall pine trees in the front yard. The string of white lights I put up two weeks ago around the front window is blinking. They look lonely and sad compared to the light display across the street, where each edge of the house is lined in every colored light imaginable. At night I am sure it is blinding. In the neighbor's front yard there is a large plastic Santa in a big red sled with Rudolf in front with his red flashing nose, and a big snowman with a real, red knit scarf around his neck and a matching hat on his head. It still does not feel like Christmas morning even with the display. I pull around to the back. My father's old, blue Ford has been parked there since Steven and I picked it up from the police impound six years ago.

My mother meets me at the top of the steps of the back door. She is disheveled and I can smell liquor masked by mouthwash, confirming she has been drinking since our phone conversation last night. I curse under my breath. I am angry. Angry at God. My heart sinks. I was hoping it would be a good day for her, but I can tell it is not going to be. My anger shifts from God to myself. I am disappointed in myself that I even hoped she would be sober on Christmas. But as much as I want to, I can not blame her, not on Christmas Day. Then I realize: I am just like her—living on hope.

Her arms flaccidly reach out to hug me.

"You're here. My beautiful boy is here!"

"Hello, Mother. Merry Christmas."

She weakly holds on to me as if she is sinking into me. She feels lifeless.

"I've been up all night making all your favorite things … there is a turkey breast, stuffing, and a whole batch of Alaskan cookies. Your favorite," she takes delight in telling me.

She is still holding on to me and I think she will never let go.

"Oh, let me get some things out of the car," I tell her.

My mother's arms slide down and rest at her hips. She steps back into the doorway. She coughs. It is a cigarette cough. I grab the presents and carry them into the house.

"Are all those for me?"

"Who else would they be for?"

She smiles and coughs again.

"And I have presents for you," she tells me.

"Socks and underwear," I think. It is always socks and underwear whether it is Christmas or my birthday. But I am fine with that. I know she wants me to always have clean socks and underwear.

"You're not going to make me wrap my own presents again, are you?"

"No. I got Siggy to wrap them when she stopped by last night. She brought me a pretty blouse and a fruit cake. But I do have some for you to wrap. Just a few, little token gifts for some of the ladies at Sunday school."

"Mom?"

"Well, you definitely have a knack for picking paper and ribbon. They're always too pretty to open. Wish I could wrap as good as you do, Son."

I laugh.

She always made good use of my talents for gift wrapping. Every year when I came home for Christmas, she would ask me to wrap all the presents she was giving. So I knew it was coming. She even had me wrap a few of my own over the years. On the holidays she was visiting me, Mother would pack the items in her suitcase and insist I wrap them once she arrived.

She walks over to the stove to check on the Stove Top Stuffing.

Yum, fruit cake, I think to myself.

"Well, thank God for Siggy."

"Oh, and I made giblet gravy," she tells me.

I look for a place to put the presents down. The kitchen table is cluttered with papers, mail, dishes; all around the small plastic Christmas tree I got her two weeks ago, too. I set them on a chair instead.

"Come open your presents," I tell her.

"Now?"

"Yes, why not? It's Christmas after all. Now is as good of a time as any."

I know she has a glass of something hidden in the cabinet above the sink. I want to distract her. She has opened it twice since stepping into the kitchen, and I know she is not looking for spices.

"Just a second."

She walks around the divider between the kitchen and the breakfast room and takes a seat at the table. Her hands are in her lap doing the finger and thumb thing. I hand her the largest present first—the dress.

"So pretty. You're such a good wrapper. Don't know where you got that talent from? It certainly wasn't from me," she comments again.

We both laugh a little. It is a nice break to the tension. She gently slides the bow and attached ribbon off the box.

"This one's a keeper," she says, as she tries not to mess it up.

She sets the bow and ribbon aside, before tearing through the silver foil paper with embossed snow flakes like a little kid would.

She pulls the box open and divides the tissue paper.

"I love it. Oh, sweetie, thank you," she says with a slight slurring in her speech. My mother pulls the dress from the box and holds it up in front of her.

"I'll have to wear this out somewhere special....You have to open one from me."

Admiringly she puts the dress back in the box and sets it on the floor before reaching across the table for a foot-long flexible package that bends in the middle as she picks it up from under the little tree. The wrapping paper, befitting a child's gift, is red, covered in reindeer with bells in their antlers. I can tell it is a package of socks by the long, soft wrapping. I act surprised and thrilled with the assortment of brown, black and blue dress socks.

"I can really use these, Mother. I have a hole in the ones I am wearing now," I lied.

"That's good. I'm glad you like them."

Mother opens two more of her presents with some delight, but I have saved the best for last: The bottle of Chanel No. 5 disguised in a larger box. Her face lights up when she discovers it is perfume. For her, Chanel No. 5 epitomizes all that is beautiful and elegant.

"And I thought you forgot. But you remembered....

You're so sneaky."

The smile lingers on her face as she opens the bottle and sprays a little on her wrists, then shrugs her shoulders in a gleeful manner. I put my new assortment of socks and another opened package of underwear back near the tree. We spend the next few hours lying on her bed watching the television. Her room is cluttered with clothes but I can tell she made an attempt to straighten things up before my arrival. She hates it when I flip the channels. There is a smorgasbord of Christmas movies, including *We're No Angels* with Humphrey Bogart, *The Bishop's Wife* with Cary Grant, *Miracle on 34th Street*, *It's a Wonderful Life*, *Christmas in Connecticut* with Barbara Stanwyck, and, of course, several versions of *A Christmas Carol*. It is obvious Mother loves movies and movie stars by how she is mesmerized by them on the television.

"I had a signed picture from Cary Grant, you know," she says as his face fills the television screen. "I was a member of his fan club when I was a girl. I had autographed pictures of all the stars."

She pauses for a minute.

"Not sure what happened to them."

"You should've been a movie star," I tell her.

"You think?"

"Of course. You're as pretty as any of them."

My mother cocks her head a little and looks off to the side.

"I guess so."

"I know so, Mother. You certainly are."

We watch *The Bishop's Wife* and then catch the last few minutes of my favorite, *Rudolf the Red Nose Reindeer*.

Later in the afternoon we eat our Christmas dinner at

the breakfast table with the little plastic Christmas tree.

"You want to drive around after it gets dark and look at the Christmas lights?" I ask her.

"Sure. I want to lay down for a bit and rest first."

"I'll take a nap myself after I clean up the dishes," I tell her.

"Thank you, Son."

My mother retires to her bedroom. I clean up the dishes and do a few other things around the house that she has neglected. Every time I come home I sweep and mop the floors, collect the trash, and go through the mound of junk mail on the table by the front door. But on each visit there seems to be more and more things to clean.

One hour later I peek into my mother's room.

"Are you sleeping?" I whisper.

"No, not yet."

"You okay?"

"I'm okay if you're okay," she tells me.

"You know what I mean."

"I'm fine. Just thinking about when you all were little."

"Oh."

"Your brother came by yesterday and dropped off a sweater and some holiday sweets from him, Rachel and the babies."

"That was nice."

"I guess."

"What are they doing today?"

"Steven said Rachel and the kids were going to her mother's house. He was going to spend the day resting. He's always working at one of those restaurants non-stop, I guess. Your sister said she would call sometime today."

"How's the Army treating her in Germany?"

227

"Good, I think. She calls every week. I got some chocolates and a nice pair of shoes from her on Tuesday."

"Well, that's good. I'm going to lay down now, and then we'll check out the Christmas lights around town."

"Okay, Son."

I lay down in the bed in my old room. I just want to get back to Atlanta, and I feel guilty for wanting to leave. But I know I have to hold out until tomorrow. The sky is growing dimmer outside and I can see the light show across the street seeping through the transparent window covering. Within minutes of lying down, I hear my mother getting up and walking into the kitchen. I know she is after the glass of whiskey hidden away in the cabinet behind the box of Cheerios. I hope she does not detect I watered it down along with the bottle I found tucked away in the back of the cabinet under the sink when I was washing the dishes. I am still exhausted from staying out late the night before and just the fact that I would rather be someplace else—a happier place. I close my eyes, but can not fall asleep. I hear my mother light a cigarette and then the sound of the cabinet door close. A few puffs later, I hear her walk back to her room. She gets up several more times over the next hour. I just lay there watching the colored lights flashing. They get brighter as the sky darkens.

Another hour passes and I have not heard my mother venture back out of her room for the whiskey for at least half that time. I quietly get up to check on her. The door to her room is partly closed. I peek in.

"You awake?" I whisper.

She does not answer. I take a few steps into the room to stand over the bed. I see her chest drawing in breath and expelling it. I can smell the liquor. Her room almost directly faces the neighbor's front yard with the over-the-top

Christmas display. I walk to the window to look at the Santa and the Snowman, and notice there is fake cotton-like snow around them. It is starting to drizzle again and a fog is collecting in the air. I find myself wishing for real snow and a real Christmas. Perhaps next year, I tell myself. I decide to let her sleep. And, we will drive around looking at the Christmas lights next year, too.

Straight Jacket

It is Wednesday. I took the day off from Macy's to head down to Warner Robins to drive Mother to see Dr. Sikes, her psychiatrist, in Macon. She still has refused to learn how to drive despite my encouragement. One of her friends, Abigail Thomson, from church, usually takes her to the standing, monthly appointment, and then they go to lunch at the Plantation House, conveniently a few blocks from the doctor's office. But they are not talking this week. Mother has been thinking everyone at church has been saying bad things about her behind her back: in particular, that she has been entertaining male visitors at home. Mrs. Thomson told Mother that it was not true, but she still thinks otherwise. Mother has spent the last week calling some of the church members, and had gone as far as calling Minister Bowman, yelling and screaming at him to make them stop telling lies about her. In our phone conversations, it has been very apparent Mother is on edge, with anxiety levels at an all-time high. Last month, she was convinced my sister's estranged husband was hiding out in the living room waiting for Sandra to come home for a visit and kill her for the insurance money. It was not the first time she had paranoid thoughts about him. A year before, when my sister was coming home on leave from Germany, Mother called the airline telling them she was afraid that Sandra's estranged husband had put a bomb in her suitcase, resulting in the authorities at the Frankfurt International Airport searching her bags and conducting a body strip search.

Not long before that she had been calling me in the middle of the night going on and on about stuff from the past and her delusions. I finally had to unplug the phone. The next morning, two Fulton County Sheriff's Deputies were knocking at my door telling me Mother had called them because I was strung out on drugs in my apartment. I am worried she will have to go back into the hospital if she does not get over these paranoid thoughts and afraid she is never going to get better. I have been in Atlanta for almost ten years. The drinking binges are getting worse and not helping the situation and I know she has not been taking her medications. In an effort to help her, months before, I purchased a weekly pill box so she could ration out her daily medications in hopes that it would be easier for her to take the correct amounts at the right times. I set up the first week's worth of pills, following the directions on the prescription bottles, but she told me she knew how to take her medications without my interference. I felt our relationship was becoming more and more strained, and the more I tried to help, the worse it was getting. I started resenting her. I had my own life to live, my own hopes and dreams, but they were for years overshadowed by her misery, and certainly, by my own problems, too. I had yet to have one good relationship with a man and had not felt the love from another human being that I had longed for until I met Christopher. I did not want fortune or fame, just to look into another man's eyes and see love looking back at me. I was living two separate lives and in two very different worlds. One was my mother's insanity and the other holding on, waiting for hope to shine through.

Mother was still bagging at the Commissary four days a week with Siggy. Siggy called me to inform that she had smelled alcohol on Mother's breath several mornings when she had picked her up. She also told me that on one of those occasions her blouse was obviously on backwards and Mother had seemed very disoriented.

Mother was waiting for me at the bottom of the back door steps holding a brown paper lunch-sack when I drove the car around. This signaled me that she did not want me to come into the house because it was in chaos. I had been concerned on the drive down of the state I might find her in, as well as the house, but I also knew she usually was on her best behavior when it was the day to see the doctor. She did not want him to put her back into the hospital.

Despite her arthritic knees, she jumped into the car before I had a chance to turn off the ignition and get out to greet her.

"Are we in a hurry?" I asked.

"No. Not really. I just was watching for you at the front window."

"Okay."

"I packed you a little snack for the drive, like I used to when I fixed your school lunches way back when."

"Thanks. That was very sweet of you."

"There's an apple and a granola bar for you, and some of those mixed nuts you like. They had them on sale in the scratch-and-dent section at the Commissary yesterday."

I backed out of the driveway and headed down Shirley Drive, before turning on Rumble Street along the high school toward Watson Boulevard. Mother fidgeted in her seat.

"I'm so over those people at the church," she offered out of nowhere.

"So, they're still talking about you?" I humored her.

"They won't stop. I'm not going back to that church."

"But I thought you were making some nice friends there. And didn't you host the picnic for the kids a few months back in the church's play ground?"

"Yes."

"I'll find another church. Bobby Gene at the Commissary wants me to go to Sunday school at her's."

"Which one?"

"Southside Baptist."

"Really."

"Yes, really."

She folded her arms across her chest like she meant business.

"Have you talked to Abigail since your fight?"

"No. And I don't plan on it!"

"Mother, I thought you two were such good friends."

"We were until she started taking up for those people at the church."

"Mother. Are you sure they were talking about you, or was it something you just got messed up?"

"Randy! Don't you start on me, too!" she crossly yelled out.

"I'm not."

"None of you children understand me!"

The years to follow were not much different; countless trips driving back and forth between Atlanta and Warner Robins. As the miles piled up, we began growing farther and farther apart. In the meantime, I somehow managed to establish myself as an artist and writer, and made several trips out to California for visits, while not much had changed with my mother. She did come up to Atlanta for the publishing party of my first book, *In the Arms of Adam: a diary of men.* It was the happiest I had ever seen her, roaming in and out of the large crowd of people, telling everyone the author was her son. Then she went on a two-week drunk after reading it, calling me on the phone one night mad as the devil.

"How could you write all those lies and half-truths about us?"

"Mother. They are the truth. You just won't admit or face them."

The years continued to blur by. At thirty-nine I was a well-grown man no longer a little boy, but I felt like one on the inside as I drove from Atlanta, this time to Milledgeville, Georgia to the State mental hospital, where my mother had been committed by court order. I remember the air was thick as the heat of the Devil's breath with the top down on my Alfa Romeo, the swirling air blowing my hair in every direction. There is nothing around me except slight hills and flat land on either side of the road. The car zooms through a grove of tall, limberly oaks forming a tunnel out of nowhere; the light quickly dims with streaks of sun stretching through the limbs onto the road and the car until it comes out the other end to bright light again and more flatness. I narrow my eyes to adjust to the intensity of the sun beating down. I am going to visit my mother, again. I have lost count of the mental wards in the various hospitals, but I no longer have to wait in the car as I did on those many occasions as a child. Just recently, she had been released from a private hospital after her insurance ran out. They packed her bag and set Mother outside to be picked up. Later that night, she made threatening calls to people she believed had wronged her. One of them called the police. When the law enforcement showed up, Mother had barricaded herself in the house—telling them she had a gun and that she would shoot anyone who tried to get her. She kept them at bay, throughout the night, until they broke into the house at 7 a. m.

I do not know this woman anymore. She is not the one who gave birth to me, or at least does not seem, act, or even look like the beautiful loving mother I remember. The years have taken her from me. Her medical report is inches thick—years of compiled reports regimentations, evaluations that read like a psychiatric text book: 53 years old, widowed, husband committed suicide in their home while she was present, mother of three children, two sons, one daughter of adult age, 12th grade education, unemployed, white female, chronic schizophrenia, bipolar, acute alcohol abuser, paranoid toward neighbors; calls the local police to get them out of her driveway and from the trees in her yard. Patient has delusions, agitated behavior. Past Psychiatric History: given electric shock therapy in intervals of every six months and given Thorazine and Stelazine. Can be hostile at times. Patient represents a threat to herself and others. At times she is delusional, referential, persecutory ideations, unable to care for herself, not eating, quite agitated, angry, threatening family members, police officers, and church members. Believes others are trying to poison her.

I arrive at the hospital waiting for her in a bland receiving room where two visitors are there to see other patients. I can tell they are not together; they are not talking to each other and no one is looking anyone in the eyes. The room is big enough to give some privacy, filled with simple faux brown leather upholstered chairs, round tables, prints of faded flowers in simple black, thin frames on the walls. I continue to wait, wondering where the years have gone, and with them my dreams of moving to California, of finding true love, of being happy.

Past visions of my mother keep entering my mind from her previous stays in the hospital. I am looking through a ten-inch by ten-inch square window of a white door; looking at my mother lying on her back on a thin mattress in a sterile room. The off-white canvas straight-jacket has her arms strapped across her chest. She is out of her mind. Literally. The room is cold and whiter than the jacket. A nurse blends into the walls with her uniform of a similar shade, as she discards the needle, just used to inject my mother with a heavy sedative, into the waste container hanging on the wall. My mother's head is shaking repeatedly back and forth as her feet are rapidly moving sole over heel, sole over heel.

"What are you doing to me? Please let me out of here," she asks in a child-like tone.

"You'll be fine, Dear," the nurse says out of habit.

"But I don't belong here!"

It is my fault that she is here now in the State Hospital. I gave up on her; gave up on any chance that she would be "normal or sane" again, like I remembered her when I was that little boy holding her hand, walking down the dirt road between the cotton fields covered in white. I had given up on trying to keep her house clean on my weekend visits. Instead, on one of those visits home I walked into the house and immediately walked back out and drove to the drug store to get a disposable camera. I returned to the house and took pictures of the deplorable conditions: piles of empty alcohol containers and decomposed food all over the house resulting in roaches crawling over every surface. Then I called my brother and told him I could not do this alone anymore. He stepped in and was appointed her legal guardian. At the custody hearing it was determined that Mother was incapable of managing her estate and lacked sufficient understanding and the capacity to make significant and responsible decisions concerning her person and property. For the next three years she became a resident of Central State Hospital. She blamed me for having her put there. I felt guilty, but I was not moving back to Warner Robins. I would rather die instead of returning to the misery from which I had come; the misery that had become a part of my being.

An elderly man in a faded brown robe walks into the visiting room and sits down beside one of the visitors. A few minutes later, my mother turns the corner. She stops just inside the entrance when she sees me, like she knows me from somewhere but is not sure where. She stands there for a minute. I can see her mind working as her eyes focus on me. She walks toward me. Stands in front of me for a second or two before sitting down.

"Hello Mother. How are you today?" I asked.

"Why did you take those pictures?" she would ask me on every visit.

"Because I didn't know what else to do. Because I love you and you need the help that I couldn't give you."

Straight Jacket

"I don't belong here. I don't belong here," she tells me over and over.

"But the doctors and the court say otherwise, Mother."

"Take me out of here. Take me home with you." She begged.

I saw a tear drop swell in her right eye.

"I wish I could, Mother. I wish I could have made you better, but it is beyond me."

"What did you do this morning?" I ask, trying to change the subject.

"They gave me a pass to go to the library. They have record albums besides books. I go almost every day and listen to the records or read the books."

"That's good, Mother."

"But I want to go home. I want to go back to my house."

"When they say you're well enough. I'm trying to get it all cleaned up for you and get it ready. Steven is taking care of the bills as the court ordered."

"Don't throw anything away. You hear me. Don't throw any of my things away."

"Of course not, Mother. I'm just getting it cleaned up. I'm not throwing anything away. Don't worry yourself. Just get better."

But I was throwing things away, but nothing I thought was important to her. It was mostly years of old newspapers and overflowing mounds of months and months of junk mail. Just like when I came home on the weekends to clean up the house before she was committed, I took trash bag after trash bag to the dumpster in back of the high school so Mother would not drag them back in from the street into the house; afraid I had thrown something of importance away.

239

"They say the next time I come I can get a pass and take you to lunch off campus if you continue to do well."

"I would like that."

"Me too, Mother."

"Are you making any friends here?" I ask her.

"Not really. They're all crazy. They do crazy things. Half of them just walk around or sit in the community area talking to themselves. Some play board games or do puzzles, but I don't like board games. Puzzles are okay. I would rather just go to the library. At least I have that."

"Do you need anything?'

"Yes! I need to get out of this place!"

"I know, Mother. I know. You will."

"Then why did you children put me here?" she asks again.

"Mother, we didn't. We want you to get well and out of here as well."

We had the same conversation visit after visit. After the first year I was able to take her off campus for a few hours. We would sit at a restaurant in the small town of Milledgeville and have long lunches. Almost every time she would ask if she could have a beer or glass of wine.

"No," I would tell her. "If the hospital staff finds out, they will not let me take you off the grounds. Do you want that to happen?"

"But, I'm not really an alcoholic."

"Mother, please don't ask me again."

Then I would change the subject.

Almost three years later, for the last time, she walked out of the white heavy metal double doors of the ward that had been her reluctant home. While she was confined, she had her knees replaced with prosthesis, allowing her to walk better than she had in the previous ten years.

I took her by the hand as we walked to the car. Half way to the parking lot, she stopped, turned around and looked at the massive white building, all the windows and terraces covered in chain-link fencing.

"I'm never going back there. Never," she informed me.

I started up the car. A song she was familiar with was playing on the radio. Mother started humming along to it.

"Yes, I'm never coming back to this place. Take me home, Son."

I did just that, took her back to the house that had been cleaned up for her return.

She lived there alone, and a year later she got Denny. Six years later, Sandra retired and moved in with Mother. I started making my plans to finally move to California. Then Mother had the first heart attack. The list of ailments grew: congestive heart failure; chronic obstructive pulmonary disease associated with her years of cigarette smoking; severe arthritis and stenosis of the spine; extreme fluctuations in blood pressure; and bouts with kidney failure. But, she was home.

Rabbit On A Stick

Almost every year they come up early despite the erratic southern winter weather—the daffodils. It has been the same occurrence as long as I can remember. Following a few days with freakish temperatures in the sixties or low seventies, after weeks of cold, sometimes frigid February weather, the tiny tips of their green stems began to peek up among the lethargic, wintering brown grass. The warmth of the sun heats up the ground where they sleep just enough to awaken them, and, within a few days, the straight and rigid stems of the daffodils begin to uncompromisingly push their way upward. Then, another exhale of winter's breath screams over them, but they remain, resolute over the cold. And, after years of doing so, they have taken over a good part of the front yard, migrating far from the flowerbed from which, as a young boy, my mother and I had first planted them.

For my mother, seeing their bright yellow blooms at the end of winter was a sign of hope that spring was on its way and that the loneliness amplified by the cold would soon be gone. Not as soon as she may have liked, but all the same, soon enough. Once the weather began to prematurely warm, my mother would stand at the window daily looking for them—looking for their green tips and the hope that the daffodils brought.

Even though the house with the daffodils is no longer my mother's, and I have no reason to return, not even to see the daffodils that cover the yard, something inside tells me that they will go on and continue to defy the cold in the years to come, and that the hope they brought my mother will be someone else's.

My mother held on to that hope until the very end. She held on to it firmly, with white knuckles, until the blood was squeezed from her hands by the sheer strength of her grip on life. For her, it was like climbing a rope without gloves; unfortunately, she kept looking downward, looking to see if misery was still in pursuit. Even in the end, when my brother, sister and I had to make the atrocious decision to have the life-support pulled from her body, she still held on to that hope; dangling from the rope of life for four more days.

I was relieved when my mother made it to her 75th birthday in August, 2006. Unfortunately, on a day that should be filled with joyous activities, I drove her, accompanied by my sister, to the hospital, where Mother had to have yet another test done. Even aided by a walker, she could hardly take three steps without becoming exhausted, forcing her to stop, her hands holding as tightly on to the handgrips as she did life. At one point, we had to hold her up to keep her from falling. My heart sank in my chest as I felt how frail her body was in my arms; the body that once carried me into this world. It was past heartbreaking to see her that way. I felt like a helpless spectator. I could only imagine what her long drawn-out days and nights were like the last year, hospitalized so many times. The physical pain was obvious. During my visits, I could hear the occasional outburst of screams, and see how they clouded her eyes. Then she went into the hospital two more times between September and that fateful November. The last time, she was rushed to the emergency room in the middle of the night after Sandra found her on her bedroom floor unable to catch her breath.

As I drove back down to Warner Robins, just a few weeks before Thanksgiving, something Mother had once told me after she had come back from a church trip to Florida, where the group had stopped at a race track, came to mind. "Hope is a funny thing," she said. "It's like the rabbit on the stick the Greyhounds chase at the racetrack. Around and around it goes—the rabbit—never getting anywhere, never making any progress....You might think that it's the rabbit that is hope," she said. "But it's rather something that lives inside the spirit of the dogs that chase it. The rabbit sparks something inside of them that makes the dogs run in circles, optimistic they will obtain hope, whatever it may be."

I was looking for any kind of hope that she would be home for the holidays. She always seemed to rally back time and time again.

I stopped just outside of the doorway of the hospital room trying to put on a happy face. There were beeps going off in the background from a monitor in the room next

245

door and a patient calling for a nurse across the hall. A
flower delivery man, carrying a large arrangement of pink
and white, was entering another room at the end of the
corridor, as a female orderly pushed a cart with sheets and
towels in my direction. My mother was lying in the bed
rubbing her feet together under the top sheet and doing the
finger thing as she watched the television anchored on the
wall with the sound turned low.

I took a deep breath and walked in.

"Okay, enough of this Mother. We're getting you out
of here. Thanksgiving is just around the corner and we're
doing dinner at my house, but of course you'll have a lot
of cooking to do."

"Is that so?" Mother said, attempting to smile.

"Yes. It won't be Thanksgiving without your famous
giblet gravy."

She snickered.

"And, then there's Christmas. We should go somewhere."

"Like where?"

"Where do you want to go?" I asked.

"Home is fine. I just want to go home....But, maybe
we can go somewhere in the Spring after," she said.

"After the daffodils come up," I thought to myself.
"Where do you want to go?"

She thought for a moment. I could almost see her
brain thinking.

"Back to The Big Easy," she said, with a hint of a
smile on her face.

"New Orleans?"

"Oh, yes."

"Have you been there?"

"I indeed have."

"When?"

"Your father and I went for a weekend after we first got married."

I was taken by surprise. She had not talked about him in the last few years.

"I didn't know that. So, you have been there once."

"Well, twice actually."

"When was that?"

"Remember when you drove to Warner Robins to take me to the Greyhound Bus station when"—she paused to catch her breath—"I went to my high school reunion?"

"Ah, yes. That was six or seven years ago?"

"Seven."

"But Fayette is a ways from New Orleans."

"Well, true," she said.

My mother paused again for a moment. She swallowed and a pained look swept across her face as her eyes closed.

"Are you okay?"

"I'm fine."

She opened her eyes and continued her story.

"Your uncle dropped me off at the bus station in Columbus, Mississippi, on the Monday evening after the reunion weekend to catch a ten o'clock bus. I remember he had just gotten back from playing golf. We had gotten up early that day to run around town.... It was like being back on the farm when I was a little girl getting up way before the sunrise every day to do my chores before catching the bus to school. One of the buses outside the station was getting ready to head out to New Orleans. I just had this wild hair of wanting to go back to New Orleans. To see if the little bistro where your father and I ate was still there."

I felt my eyes tear up as she was telling me the story. She continued.

"So, I asked the man at the ticket counter when it was leaving. Well, it was leaving in fifteen minutes. I had over an hour wait for the bus back home. So, I just changed my ticket to come back by way of New Orleans."

"Wow, Mom. That was pretty adventurous and spontaneous!"

"Yeah. I used to be. Did I ever tell you the story about how I sang with Gene Autry?"

"Ah, about a million times."

She looked out the hospital window, but further. Further than I knew I could see at that moment. She was looking back in time. Looking back to happier moments. Moments that were her's and her's alone.

"Right, of course. I guess I have."

"I'm sure that was a very exciting time for you. Like when I met Cher after I first moved to Atlanta and won that contest to be a guest at her birthday party."

She laughed.

"You were so crazy about Cher when you were in high school."

"Still am."

She laughed, again.

"So, you really went back to New Orleans?"

"Yes. It's probably the only spontaneous thing I've done in the last fifty years, Son. It felt good. I was nervous, but I had to do it. I had to go. It was like something from deep down inside of me pushing me on that bus to New Orleans."

"What did you do? If I remember correctly you were gone for only four days after I dropped you at the station and headed back to Atlanta."

248

"I just stayed the rest of the day and came back on a bus late that night."

"Where did you go? I mean, what did you do for just part of the day?"

"I went to the French Quarter and found that bistro. It had a different name. I sat at a table on the sidewalk and had a glass of wine and just lived in the moment in the sun."

"You lived in the moment? I've never heard you say that before."

"Yeah, I know. I haven't lived in the moment since I met your father, or rather a few years after that. You know, we ran off to get married. We were so much in love we just had to get married. Your father was so handsome, looked just like a movie star."

"Mother, you're going to make me blush."

"Promise me something, Son."

"What's that?"

"That you'll live in the moment a lot from now on. Don't wait. Don't just dream. Live the life you want to live the best you can. I know you can. For both of us. I want you to go ahead and move to California. It's your dream, Son."

"I'll move when I know you're okay. When you're well and you can come out to visit me. We have a list of things to do and see there."

"That would be nice. I want you to take me to see where all the stars lived. You promised—especially Rock Hudson. What a waste. To be gay and so good looking."

I laughed.

"Guess it depends on what side of the fence you're on."

"Yeah. I guess so," Mother said.

I really did not know what to say. I was in shock. This was a different woman lying in the hospital bed telling me all those things. This was not the woman I knew as my mother the past few years. But I was happy she was saying the things she was. Then I realized. It was her younger self talking. This was Mary Ellen, the young woman just off the cotton farm seeing a new life in front of her. Telling me not to make the same mistake she did. Not to lose my hopes and dreams. Telling me to live my life and not to wait.

Sandra walked back into the room from smoking a cigarette.

"Did I miss anything? Has the doctor been in yet?"

"No. We're just talking," Mother said.

Sandra looked at me.

"Yeah. Just reminiscing."

We watched Mother's eyes close, then open and close again. A low whimpering sound left her, filling the sterilized hospital room. It was the sound of life that was leaving; exiting her exhausted, sick body like dripping water from a broken spigot, and there was nothing I could do to stop the leakage. Her stomach was swollen, seemingly painfully so, like she was carrying a child past its term. It hurt to look at it, knowing that she had once carried three children when she was a young woman full of all those dreams, hopes and expectations that life would be good to her. But it was not. Somewhere along the way, life abandoned those dreams, hopes and expectations. I had once hoped to fulfill them for her, but even I had failed her, as well.

A few days later, she was put on life support.

Repeatedly, she bit on the breathing tube in her mouth, wanting it out, as her eyes struggled to talk for her. All I could say to her was that everything was going to be okay—that the doctor would take it out soon and she would be okay. I knew she was afraid, and she knew I knew, despite the façade of denial we had both built over the last months in a weak endeavor to protect each other from the inevitable. As the hours progressed, the façade thinned into a transparent veneer of fleeing hope. She, as I, realized time was running out. I feared there was so much she wanted to do and say, knowing the end was approaching, especially after our conversation about life. I saw it in her eyes, every possible emotion conveyed in them as they looked at me and then darted around the room and back at me again. All the things she had once dreamed of before marrying my father, before the abuse, her own alcoholism, and her journey into mental illness. Then, she slipped into a coma. As the last days came, before the coma, my impression was that her heart was filled with misgivings, as the hope that she had lived on for so many years quickly made its escape from her ailing body.

There were more tests. The doctors told us that if she was ever to wake up, Mother would be deaf, blind, paralyzed, or a combination of the three, and there was just too much brain damage, from lack of oxygen, to hope or expect anything more. Painfully, my sister, brother and I thought it was time to stop her suffering and let her go to find the peace that she so deserved. I called everyone I knew to pray for my mother. And, if they went to church, to ask the whole congregation to pray as well—to pray for a miracle. I wanted my mother to come home for the holidays. I wanted to take her on that trip to California. Several days later, my brother, sister and I made the difficult

251

decision to have the life support pulled from her body. Still, she hung on to hope, dangling from the rope of life for four more days.

Thursday night, the day after she was taken off life-support, I was trying to get comfortable in two chairs I had spread out in against the wall of Mother's hospital room, with a pillow and a blanket. She had been having seizures most of the night. Some were so bad that they shook the bed. Sandra was in bed with Mother as she had been night after night. I would get up when they began so I could put my hand on Mother's forehead and hold her hand. I would talk to her, telling her she was going to be okay. I was still hoping for a miracle. The seizures made her body pull into its core and her hands would clinch into fists. Although I knew they were involuntary movements, I wanted to feel her squeeze my hand as she had done so many times in my life. I can remember telling her, over the years, she would squeeze too hard and that it hurt. Mother's response was always, "Well, that's just how much I love you, until it hurts." Later, the seizures lessened, and my sister was able to fall asleep.

We had insisted that Mother be put on two very powerful IV drips which were started thirty minutes before being taken off life-support and were to be continuous to the very end. After being on so much medication over the years, she had developed a high tolerance to them. We wanted to be sure Mother felt no more pain. After the seizures subsided for awhile, I think I nodded off around 3 a.m. What seemed like just seconds later, I noticed some movement in the bed. At first, I thought it was my sister repositioning herself, but when I looked closer, I saw Mother sitting up in bed with her back to me and looking out at the scattered lights in the nightscape framed by the window. She then slowly and carefully—as if not to disturb my sister's sleep—got out of bed. Mother then walked around the bed toward my make-shifted one, and stopped in front of me for a moment. She put her hand on my shoulder. I looked into her eyes—clear as the water in a mountain stream. Then she spoke to me.

"Don't worry. I'll be right back, Son."

My eyes followed her. She pushed the door open and proceeded to walk out of the ICU room. I guess I was dreaming, but it felt like it was so real and I was awake. I truly believe Mother's spirit left her body that night. Now, she was unchained from the hospital bed and the confining walker she had so often used to take small, calculated steps across the room.

On Saturday, November 18, 2006, on what would be her last day on earth, some of Mother's favorite music, by Anne Murray, was softly playing non-stop on a small C D player positioned on the ledge of the window. The day before, I had bought a spool of hunter-green—her favorite color—braided ribbon to make friendship bracelets, one for mother and one for everyone who came to see her to symbolize how we are all tied together to hope. In the early evening, JoAnn brought a special cross. We each held it in our hands and said a prayer, before JoAnn placed it under Mother's left hand.

That evening, the seizures started up again, coming every thirty minutes or so. Around eight p.m., Mother had a really bad episode. I immediately reached for her hand. Afterwards, I noticed that her labored breathing had slowed. The nurse had earlier turned off the monitors in the room because they were going off all the time as Mother's vital signs were weakening. She was still able to

253

monitor Mother from the nurses' station outside the ICU room. I went out to ask her how much time she thought we had with her. The nurse believed Mother would go that night, if not by sometime in the early hours of the morning. But, I knew in my heart that she had already left the night I saw her get out of the hospital bed and look me in the eyes as she walked out the door. I returned to my chair next to the bed and sat silently as my sister continued talking non-stop to JoAnn, mostly out of nervousness.

As the night progressed, I noticed another change in Mother's breathing. It was becoming weaker and weaker, and the time between breaths was growing longer and longer. I looked at the clock on the wall. It was 11:54pm. I stood up and put my hand on my sister's shoulder.

"Be quiet," I told her.

Sandra, JoAnn and I looked at Mother as she struggled to take another breath, and then she exhaled. I waited for her chest to rise, but it would be her last one—she was gone. Just minutes before midnight, I witnessed the woman who gave me life 51 years ago take her last breath as a mortal—the last inhalation of hope. For a second I felt a sense of relief that Mother's pain was finally over before a massive wave of sadness crashed over me. Nothing could have prepared me for that moment or the pain that took over my heart and gripped my soul. After the wave passed, the emptiness it left was indescribable. Whatever that was the rabbit had that sparked hope in the Greyhounds had left my mother's body, but the hope that the daffodils bring will always be a part of me, as it was my mother.

Until Death You Do Part

They are both gone now: their bodies will soon be lying in the same hole in the cool, late November ground. The sun shown brightly in the lucid sky, but it was too distant to completely warm the day of such a reunion. A forlorn chill in the air persistently encircled me, as I stood like a statue looking at the mound of clay-colored dirt excavated from the grave that had for years cradled my father's coffin, concealing the relinquishing, quiet decay of his body. Now, the earth had been opened up again to welcome another. After his departing thirty-four years ago, my parents are reunited. I wonder what they would think, now that their human remains will be stacked together— hers over his—sharing a single white marble headstone in the formal, military graveyard. It was a hard decision to make to

put her body there, and the reality at that moment of seeing the dirt and the hole in the earth made me realize that
they are together forever—this time around.

It is a reunion of sorts for me with my father as well. I
had not ventured back to his grave since the day his body
was lowered into the ground and I heard twenty-one bullets ring out in succession—making three loud shots—
shooting up into a cloudless blue October sky. As the sub-
sequent years collected, I forced myself to forget any
dates associated with him, including his birthday. They
came and went with no outward remembrance—Father's
Day, Thanksgiving and Christmas the same, no remembrance. But, we are forced to meet once more at the very
place I said goodbye. If not for that day—my mother's
funeral—I would have never walked on the same ground
again as long as I lived. That day, I was reminded why she
was the way she was; why she became a living corpse.
Now, she would be entombed with him.

If there had not been outside influences in making the
decision for her final arrangements, I would have cre-
mated my mother's body and, in a symbolic gesture, freed
her once and for all from the grip of all the things that
held her captive in life. I might have taken some, a small
portion, perhaps a handful, of her ashes and gently sown
them over the grass covering his grave, and watched them
settle between the short, green blades for their early years;
for the time that they thought they were truly and completely in love. Then, I would have boarded a plane for
California with the rest of my mother's remains. Across
the country we would have flown, finally taking that trip I
had promised her when she had recovered—to the place I
had dreamed about since I was a teenager and had escaped
to for periods of time in my adult life. I would have taken

her to all the places I love: to the mountains and ocean of the west. We would have walked over the sand and felt the water lap at our bare feet, feeling the heartbeat of the earth. And, of course, to the places she had dreamed of seeing since she was a little girl: to the homes where all the movie stars that she had idolized from her childhood had lived, to see the Hollywood sign, and to Grauman's Chinese theater to walk among the famous signatures, foot and handprints of those idols.

I would have driven us along the Pacific Coast Highway. We would have had a long-overdue conversation, one-sided of course, but at least it would have been a conversation, and I would have finally gotten everything off my chest that had been weighing me down—laboring my breathing for so many years. I would tell her everything I had never told her about myself, including all the things she never wanted to know, or was afraid of knowing. I would tell her that I understood her madness, that it was inside of me as it was in her and that I have stopped blaming her for the madness and the drinking. That I understand she was lashing out at my father and at the lost dreams and not at me. I would tell her about all the times I prayed to God to turn back the years so that she could have had a different life and that I would have freely traded mine for a better one for her. I would tell her how much I love her, not loved, and how grateful I am she gave me life.

I would have driven until I could not talk anymore, until my voice grew hoarse and I cried every last tear. And at the moment I believed everything had been said, every tear had fallen, I would have pulled the car over and that would have been the spot where I would have released her remains. I would have sat on the edge of the earth with her in my arms, and cradled her like she had done me, time and time again. And at that very moment—the instantaneous split second—when the sun first touched the water, spilling its blistering color into the sky, I would set her free. By doing so in such a manner, the lighted wick of her spirit, severely weakened and nearly blown out by the obstacles of her life—by events in her childhood, by my father, by his violence, by her insanity—would have regained a full flame from the sun, and would have burned brighter then ever before.

So, two weeks after her funeral, I did the next best thing. I spent hours going through the dog-eared boxes of photographs documenting the past. Images of her as a young girl full of life and hope and dreams. She was so unmistakably beautiful, so fresh and so alive. Her skin was devoid of bruises and scars then, and her heart free. Her eyes were wide and lips full to see and taste everything life had to offer. There was a future ahead of her. In the early photos, she appears so eloquent and poised. God, what happened to her? My anger billowed in my core, at the deepest part of me, that she had such an unfulfilled life. The truth is hard—past hard—to digest in my guts. I felt like I needed to vomit. My stomach began to ache for her and for those lost hopes and dreams as I scrutinized each picture; picking out the ones that appeared to mean something, and began stacking them in a pile. As the hours collected into a premature morning, the pile grew higher and higher. Many of her. One of her and my father dancing, his arm around her waist, holding her close. One of her three children standing on a playground, and another sitting with her at a picnic. And, of course, the one of her standing in a field of white.

They all brought back memories from my child's

mind: the sound of the faint echoes of her voice; a little boy's hand pulling at her skirt as I followed her around like a puppy; the sparkle in her eyes as she leaned down to kiss my cheek, leaving the soft loving imprint of red lipstick; and the lingering scent of her perfume as she walked away. Then there were the other memories: her voice liquored and with a tone of sadness, as she sat at the kitchen table singing along to old standards that were the music of her youth; the clouds of smoke from her cigarettes as they hung in the air around her like that on a stage of a theater; and the bottles of alcohol on the table, her audience; the lifeless look in her eyes; and the crazy, undistinguishable mutters of madness that seeped into the walls of the house that was more like a prison than a home.

I made copies of the collected photos representing the very best of her, and bundled the replicas in the hunter-green braided ribbon leftover from the friendship bracelets. I put the bundle of copied pictures in my backpack and boarded a Delta flight to California. I drove up the Pacific Coast Highway with the bundle on the passenger seat. I had that conversation with my mother. I pulled the car over at the very spot I felt I had said all I could but was really too tired to talk anymore and unable to see through the tears. I reached in the back seat for the simple polished silver metal box I purchased at a gift store in West Hollywood. With the box in hand, and the bundle of pictures close to my heart, I walked to the edge of the world and looked out over the ocean, greeted by a tranquil wind of hope. I estimated I had about an hour left. I found a spot to sit. I placed the bundle and the metal box side-by-side before pulling the mister of Chanel No. 5 that I took from my mother's dresser after her death out of my jacket pocket. I sprayed the remaining perfume; only a few mists

Alabama Snow

left—enough to remind me of how she smelled—over the bundle. It dribbled into the surrounding air. I pulled out the lighter, purchased where I stopped to get gas and a Diet Coke, from the pocket of my jeans.

Ceremoniously, I moved the bundle to my lap and untied the bow. Devotedly, and with tremendous regret, I viewed each picture carefully again before setting each one on fire and placing them in the box. I watched the edges burn as the fire grew into the middle until they turn to ashes—all the memories, obscured by years passed, clicked through my head like a slide show. That day, looking out over the ocean, I felt she was lovingly sitting beside me with a smile on her face. The air smelled clean and sweet, scented by smoke and Chanel No. 5.

The light over the ocean was brilliant, so unlike that of the dimness of her hospital room those final days, where she looked over at me from the bed before slipping into the coma; the breathing tube down her throat. I wiped the wetness from my cheeks as I vigilantly observed the descent of the sun, still feeling my mother sitting next to me. This time she was happy—the way I prefer to remember her. We both watched it majestically slipping downward toward the blue-green water. And, at that very moment— the instantaneous split second—when we saw the sun touch the water, spilling its blistering color into the sky, I looked into my mother's eyes and set her free. The ashes danced from the box, out over the cliff floating toward the exploding color from the sun.

It was because of that message to my father written on the back of my beloved picture of my mother—*Darling, this picture makes me appear larger than I am. Love, Mary Ellen*—that made me dismiss my own wishes for her and return my mother to him. And because of my

Mother's request thirty-four years ago, when she woke me from a troubled sleep in a house earlier shaken by a rifle shot, to take her to the funeral home so she could sit with him. Hopefully, this time, they have made peace.

Life Imitating Art

I was a vulnerable, young child, walking many fine, delicate lines, between sanity and insanity, between love and hate, between sadness and longing, optimism and dread, anger and cautioned joy, trust without questioning or foreseeing the potential consequences. I have seen the glass half empty and half full, and I have balanced on the edge separating life and death after witnessing the remains of the latter; living a fragile alliance with life itself. Elongated, crisscrossing spider-like webs, fragile lines, some thinner than others, some taut, others wobbly, but all capable of snapping at any moment in time; waiting for me to slip, to snare and entangle my soul in order to squeeze out its essence. I walked closely behind my mother as she maneuvered these divisions from the day she gave me life and until the day she died. I am as much a part of her as

263

we are both of the soil that grows the cotton. As we are of the soil, so are we of the cotton, and will always be made of its very fibers.

Insanity does run in families. To what degree I have inherited all or any part of the malady that has been carried down from generation to generation, I do not know. But, I know I have something. Whether I got it in the womb of my mother, or whether it transferred to me when I stared into her eyes on that day she was taken screaming from our house on one of her early break-downs, or whether I absorbed it from the house of violence we lived in, it has been a part of me ever since. My father's suicide opened the door to hell and the door to self destruction in all my family members' lives, as well as that one door that no one should enter, where on the other side whoever crosses its threshold ends up taking their own life. I know too well the cosmic damage such an act leaves behind.

Is it crazy to want to kill yourself? Sometimes everything seems pointless. Getting out of bed can be such an impossible feat. There have been periods when I have detested the mornings, cursed the first light introducing another day of life, another day of misery, when I know I should be grateful to have another day to live. But it is getting through the day, when each passing minute feels like I am pulling a ton of stone across the floor of life. Minutes are like hours, endless hours to survive when it seems so much more humane to just end it. End it once and for all. My father did it—killed himself and I never thought he was crazy, just mean, angry and lost. My sister has tried three times; the cuts, now scared-over, are a testament of her pain. And it even goes back further in time to my grandmother, and who knows beyond her. My mother certainly threatened to on many occasions, but I do not believe she ever really wanted to. They were her cries for help, her uproar to be noticed. The times I took her to the emergency room to have her stomach pumped, she had just messed up her medications, and, combined with alcohol, made it appear that she was trying to end her melancholy existence. But she had hope and no matter how fragile or thin that string was which tied her to it, she never wanted to let go and never wanted it to break. This is how we are different. I have wanted to let go of that string; I have wanted it to break. It is a secret I have kept hidden the majority of my years. A secret that lives and continues to grow deep down inside of me.

All my life, I have experienced the roller coaster ride from sanity to insanity. They say crazy runs in families, and it is apparent it runs in mine. But I do not feel crazy, just alone, sad, afraid and I have felt that way most of my life—so many more times than I have felt happiness. The truth is, I was not really sure what this happiness is supposed to feel like. This exhilaration, this joy, this delight of which I had thought I had found a few times in my life, but whatever the feelings were, they were short lived, slipping through my fingers like blood leaving a dying body—my dying spirit. Time and time again, I still feel like the little boy, my knees sinking into the mattress of the small twin bed, watching my parents fight over the butcher knife in the hallway bathroom of the small house on Euclid Circle; waiting for it to plunge deep into one of them. Then I met Christopher, and my body became filled with this happiness.

Before him, I have thought about killing myself numerous times in my life and more recently, even going as far as planning it out. I just did not want to leave a mess, like my father had done. I did not want someone to have to clean up the remnants of death as I had done at such a young age. I did not want someone else's hands to be stained by my blood as mine were with my father's. His blood may have appeared to be washed away from my hands, but they had been forever stained since that Fall afternoon. I can remember being in my early twenties; at a time I had everything to live for, recklessly driving my car down a deserted road late into the daunting hours of the night with a few drinks in my belly, counting the telephone poles, one, two, three, four and so on—trying to decide which one to hit. Trying to decide which one would finish the job.

I went to the doctor yesterday. It was such a beautiful day. The sun was brilliant as its light filtered through the sunroof of the Rover; a transparent yellow glaze washed over my hands on the steering wheel. It was an abnormally temperate day for the season. The sky was azure with high clouds full of shape and form like magnificent sculptures made by Michelangelo himself with the help of angels. They were glorious, but all I could think about was ending the pain in my heart that so gravely encumbered my soul—the unbearable pain—an agonizing, monstrous ache that has visited me time and time again throughout my life. I had barely survived the holidays and felt the thin string of hope becoming finer and finer as the days passed, truly believing and hoping it would snap. All the way to the doctor's office I prayed for a heart attack, a stroke, a car wreck, anything that would bring death to me in an instant.

Dr. Thomas looked up at me from the little four-legged stool with wheels as I sat up on the examining table, the white sterile paper crinkling under me as I seem unable to sit still, repeatedly running my hands through my short hair.

"What seems to be the problem?" he asked

"All I can think about is dying."

He looked at me for a second before speaking, clearly seeing how inflamed and swollen my eyes were.

"Dying as you are afraid of getting sick, or as in suicide?" he clarified.

"Suicide."

Then I started bawling as I had been in the Rover on the way in to see him. My face was washed over in tears, my lungs unable to breathe in air. I started to hyperventilate.

Dr. Thomas rolled over on the stool and put his hand on my knee.

"Deep slow breaths, Randy. What has happened to make you feel like you want to die? Do you know how many patients I see here a week that are just hanging on to life. You are perfectly healthy."

"I'm spent: emotionally, physically, spiritually. Just spent. It's a huge effort to get out of bed in the mornings. My days are empty. I'm filled with nothingness."

"But you have done so much. Your charity work, your art, the books and the new one about your mother. Why, I remember when you were here a few months back for your physical, you seemed in great spirits. You seemed so optimistic. So in love with life."

"It's all a façade. It's always been. I try to act happy on the outside, but everything inside is shit. It feels worst than shit. I have always been that way. A fake. All my life I have felt like a fake. I know the right things to say and do, but I don't know how to live them. I never have."

"Well, let me ask you something."

"Okay."

"Have you actually tried to kill yourself?"

I was quiet for a moment.

"Yes, just a few days ago. I was going to take three bottles of sleeping pills."

"Well, I can see by you being here today you thankfully didn't take them. And besides, I see in your records I have not prescribed any to you in quite some time. Where did you get the pills?"

"From my sister."

My sister had called one afternoon out of the blue. We had been estranged for a year. I was surprised to get the call. She sounded sober. Sandra told me she had not had a drink in three months. I was glad for her that she seemed to be doing better, having just finished another rehab, she told me. The next day I drove back to Warner Robins to see her, not having been back since the funeral. Sandra wanted to see me and I wanted to say goodbye. And I wanted to encourage her to keep doing better. She deserves to be happy. It is what our mother has always wanted for her and all her children—to be happy. We all went our separate ways after the funeral. But, in actuality, we had done so after our father's suicide. Sandra had moved four times since Mother's interment. She did not last very long in San Antonio, Texas. Then she moved to Fayette, thinking she would feel closer to Mother. Then to Phenix City, right outside of Columbus, Georgia, so she could go to Mother's grave daily. She would take a lounge chair and sit at the grave reading books all day until they closed the gates at five o'clock. Then, she moved back to Warner Robins.

I wanted to show her support. She had informed me she had gotten a job working with young girls at risk. I wanted someone in this family to survive. And I needed something to do; I was beginning to feel trapped in the house, unable to sit still. But, I had an ulterior motive. For years, both Sandra and my mother had given me sleeping pills from their stash. I have always had problems sleeping. During that phone conversation Sandra told me she has been saving up some pills for me—almost three prescription bottles. I go for the pills more than to see her. I see them as a possible way out.

I met my sister at the old mall parking lot just inside Warner Robins. She looked good as she got out of the car. We stood in the cold and hugged each other.

"It's so good to see you, Randy," Sandra said.

I had not seen her since she dropped me off at the San Antonio International Airport two years ago.

"Yes, good to see you, too. You look great."

"Yeah, I've cleaned up my life, thanks to God, and my new psychiatrist is wonderful. I think they both are straightening me out. But, Randy, how are you doing? You look tired."

"To be honest, I'm a mess. My boyfriend broke up with me. I feel lost without him."

"You'll be okay."

"I don't feel like I will. I miss him so much. I can't tell you how much. I'm trying to be okay, but I am lost without Christopher. Totally lost. But I'm so happy that you're doing well, Sister."

"Thanks. I know you are. I have been such a mess for so long. I still miss Mother every day."

"I know you do. Me too."

"I'm sorry you are in so much pain over this guy. I can see it in your eyes," she tells me.

"I want him back."

"Well, it can happen. Anything is possible. I will pray

for you both."

"Thank you."

I start to cry.

"You want to see my new place?"

"Yes, of course. Then we'll get some lunch."

I wipe my face of the tears of loss.

I followed my sister to her new home. It was on the other side of town from where we grew up. I did not entertain the thought of going by our last childhood house. I had promised myself the night before Mother's funeral I would never return. It was one promise I was going to keep.

Sandra was proud of her new place and excited about her pending job. She still had Dallas, her dog, older, limping, but still alive.

"Where is Denny?" I asked.

"He got left behind in San Antonio. He just ran away one day. Probably looking for Mother. I like to think he found a new home," Sandra said.

"Me too."

After the tour, Sandra wanted to head on to lunch. As we were walking toward the front door, I asked her about the pills.

"Oh. Yes, the sleeping pills. They're in the bathroom."

"How many bottles did you say you had?" I asked.

"Just under three prescription bottles," she answered. "I don't need them much anymore. The doctor has me on something for anxiety that makes me fall asleep better."

Then she looked at me funny for a minute or so.

"You're not going to do something stupid?" she asked.

"What do you mean?"

"You're not going to kill yourself, are you? You don't

look happy." Then she started to cry.

"No. Of course not. I just need to sleep. And you know how I like free stuff."

Sandra opened the medicine cabinet and pulled out the three bottles.

"Promise me you're telling me the truth."

We were both quiet for a moment. Dallas was looking at us from the bed.

"Why would I do something like that?"

"Okay, then."

She put them in a bag and reluctantly handed it to me.

"Thank you."

"Did you see the pictures of Mother on the wall?"

"How could I miss them? They look nice. She is looking down on you. She always will," I told Sandra.

"And you and Steven, too," Sandra added.

"Why did she give you three bottles of sleeping pills?" Dr. Thomas asked.

"I asked her if she had any extra. She told me she had been saving them up for me because I've had trouble sleeping over the years. Bad periods of insomnia."

"Well, I see I had prescribed some for you several years back. Why didn't you ask for more?"

"When my mother was alive, she had a virtual drug store in her house. They had been free. At the time you wrote the prescription, I was not going home for a few days and I needed them at that time. Other than that, I would get a few here and there from both my mother and sister, too."

"I've known you for a long time. I have some of your beautiful art in my home. Randy, I can assure you, you're not a fake."

"Then why do I feel like one? Like I'm nothing?"

"I can tell you are very distraught. How about if I put you in the hospital for a few days? Get you straightened out?"

"No! I won't. I can't go. I have been on the other end of that all my life with my mother in and out of mental wards. I won't go. I'm not crazy. If you try to make me, I'll leave now."

Dr. Thomas looks more concerned.

"I can force you if I think you're a danger to yourself."

"No!" I repeated as I started to get up off the table.

"Okay, Randy. Wait. Sit back down."

Dr. Thomas looked down at his computer with my records.

"Then you must promise me you'll not do anything. What about your boyfriend, Christopher is his name, right?"

I started crying again. A flash flood washed out of my tear ducts.

"Do these thoughts of suicide have anything to do with him...did you two break-up?" Dr. Thomas asked.

"He's so busy with law school. I never see him. He's getting ready to start his second semester."

"Law school is a lot of work. Grueling, I understand, almost as bad as medical school."

"He's out-growing me. It's been two years and now he has out-grown me. His life is just beginning and I feel like mine is ending. I feel like I need to end it. I feel like I have been here too long."

"Randy, I know you lost your mother not too long ago. Does the book have anything to do with your feelings as well? I know you have been digging up some troubling stuff and most likely reliving it. And didn't you meet

Christopher shortly after her death?"

"Yes. I guess. It's all too much at times. And right now I feel like everything is crashing in on me. I realize I'm just like she was—my mother. That's why we were so close and so far apart at the same time. We were mirror images inside and out of each other. And now I'm loosing Christopher, too. I love him...more than anything."

And it was true. Everything was crashing in on me. The months and months of reliving my mother's life and pain, combined with the realization Christopher was outgrowing me had taken a huge toll. He found me two years ago; just a month and a half after I buried my mother, I got a random email from him. He was afraid of facing the truth that he is gay. Sick of hearing all the gay jokes from his friends, on and off the soccer field and at home. Afraid of telling his family. He found me on one of the gay websites where I was promoting my writing. He even used a fake name, Clark as in Clark Kent, of Superman fame. He wrote: *I have a lot of concerns about my future and what kind of decisions I should make in my life. I have known I had homosexual feelings since I was about in the 6th grade but I have always kept them buried deep inside of me. However, as I get older they are getting hard to ignore. I come from a very conservative family and a conservative community and if I were to be open about being gay I would be on my own from that point onward. My whole life I have had to portray this image of domineering heterosexual masculinity but I don't know how long I can keep it up. All I want to do is just get married and have kids and lead a normal life like the majority of society, but I dunno if I can let myself live that kind of life. I don't want to meet some amazing woman and marry her and start a family and then 5 years down the road, I realize that I am*

100% gay and I have made a huge mistake. It wouldn't be ethical for me to play games with other people's lives and also to bring kids into the world would just be cruel. If I knew I could fight these urges then I would not be so worried but sometimes they just beat my will power. The one hope I have that I may yet be able to have a normal heterosexual life is that when it comes to men I'm only attracted to men older than me. I have never had any sort of sexual attraction to any of my friends or any guy that's near or around my age. I dunno where these feelings for older men come from but I was thinking that maybe it is just psychological, the fact that my father was never around when I was a kid may have made me subconsciously look for another father figure in other men. Another thing that scares me is that, although I do not have nearly any experience in the gay lifestyle, it just seems so unstable. It seems like most guys just want to screw each other and that's it. 99% of the guys that have contacted me on daddyhunt.com just talk about sex and I wouldn't want to live a life where I just float from one sexual encounter to the next. I need stability and a family to be a part of. I feel really strange about writing this email as you are a complete stranger to me but I'm telling you things that I have never uttered to anyone. You just seem like a really good guy that is sincere and caring and who is not just going to feed me a lot of bull. I read your homepage on AOL hometown and I have to say I am very impressed. Physically you look like you should be on the football field but inside you have a lot of deep amazing thoughts. The passage from your book "In the Arms of Adam: a diary of men" where you say "There are many times I laid naked beside the men in my life and felt ashamed. I felt I was a lesser person than even the men in my company. I will never again allow such thoughts, stimulated by past experiences or our suppressive and unknowing society, to enter into my mind. The comfort I seek is the comfort I require and there is no shame in any two people sharing with one another..." hit me extremely hard. That is a very powerful passage and it hits close to home with me as I have had those feelings everyday for the past 9 years, although I have only been with one man and it was nothing that got too intense I can still relate to those feelings. I intend on going to Barnes and Noble tomorrow to look for a copy. Anyway as I said before I feel a little strange writing you such a long email where I am just dumping the past 9 years of emotional baggage, but I just really needed someone to talk to and you seem like a considerate guy that could understand what I am going through. Thanks for listening.

Clark

He was me thirty years ago—except he was the athlete that no one would ever guess was gay. He was me on the inside, and bigger and stronger on the outside. It was his façade to hide what was going on inside of him, just as I had done and have been doing most of my life. We emailed back and forth for awhile and then eventually met. I was still recovering from losing my mother. Christopher made me realize that I had missed out on my youth. Five, ten, fifteen, twenty years had turned into thirty, and, before I knew it, those young years were gone—so far gone, never to be regained. Those years had moved faster than my father's speeding car over the road between the cotton fields on my grandfather's farm in Alabama. I had been too engrossed in my parents, and particularly in my mother's pain, to be fully aware of my own. Two years later, now that Christopher seemed to be moving on, that pain I had kept deep down inside for years, buried, had surfaced like an erupting volcano.

"Randy, we can get you better," Dr. Thomas reassured. "It'll take a little time, but you'll get better, you'll feel like living again. Too many people love you. Think about them."

"I do. I have, but they have no idea of the magnitude of my pain. I have never felt so much hurt, sadness and loss, and what I'm feeling would overflow the Grand Canyon. And I want to live, but not with the agonizing pain. Not with the void and not without Christopher. I feel guilty fully knowing there are sick people all over the world in hospitals dying, holding on to life like my mother did, wanting another chance to live. You don't have to tell me. I know I'm considered successful, healthy, a likable guy, even in great shape—for my age, and handsome. I have great friends, and, most of all, I finally truly love someone, Christopher, for two years now."

And, yes, I had waited fifty-one years to meet someone to truly love. It all seems like a vindictive joke. A young man has brought more joy into my life than I have ever experienced in the fifty-three years I have lived. I can remember him holding my face in his hands, telling me I could never disappoint him, that he loved me that much. In his last Valentine's Day card he wrote: You are the best thing that has ever happened to me in my life. Now, I am nothing. I was blessed, now I am cursed. I still can not stop the thoughts of death and the thoughts of him outgrowing me. How am I going to deal with all of it? Death seemed to be the only answer for me. I had to stop the demon that was overtaking my life. I had to kill it, even if it meant killing myself in the process. It just had to be a quick, easy, and clean death with no mess for anyone to clean up. I had already lain awake night after night going through the scenarios: sleeping pills; slashing my wrist in a tub of warm water; pulling my XJS into the studio among all the art I had created—finished and unfinished—leaving the car running with me sitting in the driver's seat; or driving up to the mountains and off the top of one of them; going over to visit a friend who lives in a high-rise condo on the twenty-seventh floor and jumping off the balcony when her back is turned. Or, finding a gun, but not having to wait for a permit. I had several thousand dollars in cash stashed away in the house for an emergency. But where to get it—the gun? I would open the driveway gate that led to the back gravel turnaround in front of the studio. Then I would call the police to inform them of my address and that within moments my body would be lying on the ground. I would tell them to please hurry and send someone to get my body before anyone else would see it. And to be sure to wash away the blood with the hose connected to the water spigot on the side of the house. But I could not wait any longer, wandering the streets looking for a gun—and it was too much like following in my father's footsteps if a gun were involved.

All selfish acts. And if anyone should know what a selfish, atrocious, unthinkable act killing oneself is, then I should. I still remember how I felt after my father killed himself. Even though I had said I was relieved, I was still mortified, shocked, devastated and felt deserted as I cleaned up what was left of him.

Dr. Thomas continues to stare at me like he is sizing me up.

"What about any friends?"

"Yes, I can call Mace, Nicole or Theo."

"You want me to call them?"

"No. I will."

"Promise me."

"Yes. I promise."

He continues his pep talk. Then hands me the prescription for Clonazepam and Paroxetine. I take them, but am skeptical. None of the medications seemed to have ever worked for me in the past, and I forget all the long names of the wonder drugs that I have taken on and off over the years.

"I want to see you in a week. I have also written down the name of a psychiatrist. I want you to make an appointment with. Just talk to him. He's great. Call me day or night. Okay? Lots of people love you."

"I'm not crazy. My heart is destroyed."

"I understand, Randy. Will you do what I say?"

"Okay, yes," I answered.

The String of Hope that was Always There

Christmas Day 2008 came. Christopher was home with his family. Dugan was chasing his tail on the bed next to me. The television was on low. I had seen the doctor twice since my initial appointment and still felt the same. Christopher and I had had an argument and have not talked all week. I put Dugan in his crate and drove around the city for an hour or so. The streets were empty and there were Christmas lights everywhere making me more depressed, if that was even possible. I drove back home. Got Dugan and got back into bed. I took two Paroxetine pills and finally fell asleep.

I had heard a rumor that Christopher had been on a few dates with someone from the gym. Somehow I survived through New Year's, Dugan and I. Each night, I slept on Christopher's side of the bed, holding two pillows to my bare chest. Friends invited me out, but being with them would just make me feel worse, if that were even possible. I had the means to go almost anywhere I wanted, but I could not make it past the bedroom door. I could have gone back to California, but Christopher and I had just been there before he started law school. It was heaven waking up with him in my arms each morning looking out the expansive windows of the house on the cliff at the blue sea below us. I could have gone to Spain or France or perhaps back to Italy. I had always wanted to go back, but with the love of my life—Christopher—not alone and not just anywhere I would be a stranger with no history or future—just a soul walking the earth looking for something or looking for nothing. I thought about some far-off place, remote, but realized I was already there—in a remote place.

New Year's Day I made sure that my will was in order and that all the papers were together, just as my father had done many years ago, when he had placed all his government papers and financial documents on his desk in the bedroom before returning to the living room and shooting himself.

Another week passed. Saturday morning I woke up in a panic. I desperately needed to hear Christopher's voice. I reached for my cell by the bed, scrolled down to his number. It went right to voicemail. Later that day I was suppose to help a friend, Nicole, set up for a show at one of the major hotels downtown. I got out of bed, dressed quickly and got in the Rover. I drove by Christopher's place—he had rented a house not far from mine with two of his friends from the gay soccer team. His car was parked in the back. I knocked on the door. One of his roommates came to the door to inform me he was not home. That told me he had spent the night out, probably with someone else. I got back in my Rover and drove home. I called Christopher again and left a message: "So, I guess you're really seeing someone else since you're not at home." My world crumbled under me. As I pulled into the driveway, I saw my neighbor in his front yard. He called out to me, "I saw Christopher at the Heretic last night with a good-looking guy." At that moment Nicole pulled up to pick me up. I got into her car and started crying a few seconds after she started toward downtown.

"It's over. Christopher was out all night with someone else."

Then my phone rang. It was Christopher.

"I was just out with friends. No big deal."

"I don't believe you. You were out with that guy from the gym."

"He's just a guy. He means nothing to me."

"I have to go, Christopher. I'm with Nicole. She has a show tonight."

I closed the phone and started to cry again.

Nicole did not say a word. She just kept driving.

"I can't help you today," I blurted out as she pulled up in front of the hotel. "I'm going to call a taxi to take me home."

"No. Stay with me. You're too upset. It'll just take a few minutes to go over the performance. Then I'll take you home."

I followed her into the ballroom completely in tears. Everyone around could see I was crying. I started pacing as Nicole went over to talk to the other performers. I ran out into the lobby area. A few minutes later she came looking for me.

"I have to go home! Now! I just want to die."

"Randy, get a hold of yourself. Please."

"I can't. My life is over."

"No, it's not."

"Yes, it is. I just want to see Christopher one more time. I'll call him. He'll come get me."

I rang his number while Nicole stood by in concern. Christopher answered.

"I'm at the hotel. Can you come get me?" I asked.

"Yes."

"When?"

"I'll leave now."

I looked at Nicole.

"He's on his way. I'm going outside to wait on him."

"I'll go outside with you. I don't want to leave you alone."

"No! No! I just want to be alone with him."

"I'm not letting you out of my sight."

For a second I thought about running to the elevator, taking it to the top floor and jumping, but Nicole was just inches behind me. I ran out to the street. She followed. Within a few minutes Christopher pulled up. I got into the front seat as Nicole jumped into the back.

"You have a show to finish getting ready for. Go back in," I told her.

"No, I'm going with you both. The hell with the show. You're more important."

Christopher looked back at Nicole.

"Go. Let's get him home."

Christopher pulled up into my driveway. The hotel was just a few minutes from the house.

"Nicole, take one of my cars and go back," I told her.

Christopher just sat in the driver's seat.

I opened the door and ran into the house. I went to my bedroom to get the bottles of pills out of the dresser drawer in case they tried to get them first. They both bolted out of the car behind me and into the house. I ran out the back door with the bag of pills and into my studio—looking for a place to hide them—but they both had me cornered. I started to cry out of control.

"Randy, give me the pills," Nicole demanded.

"No. Just go back to the hotel. Take one of my cars," I said again. "Or Christopher will take you."

I was out of my mind. All I could think about was losing Christopher—never being able to hold him again, or kiss him, or make love to him. Never! At that moment everything seemed so final. He was standing by the door in shock at my actions. I had always been the strong one and now he was seeing me at my worst; my most pathetic, at my weakest, most vulnerable state. I ran past them into the backyard and back into the house. I grabbed the keys to the Jag and managed to lock up the pills in the trunk. Then I ran down the street. Nicole followed. Christopher stood by his car, still in disbelief. I managed to double back to the house and to Christopher. Within seconds, Nicole was back, too. Even though Christopher's car had my Rover blocked in, I jumped into it and turned on the ignition, put the Rover in reverse and tried to push his Corolla out of the way. But he reached in and fought with me for the key. After a few moments of struggle, I gave up.

"I'll take you back to the hotel, Nicole, and stay with Randy," Christopher told her.

"Then he has to come, too. I don't want him to be alone."

"Okay. I'll come. I'm sorry," I told them ashamed.

We returned her to the event so she could get ready. I got out of the front passenger seat. She got out of the back. We hugged. I started to cry again.

"I'm sorry, Nicole. I hope I didn't mess up your event."

"No. It'll be fine. I have plenty of time. Just promise you won't do anything. That you won't take the pills."

"I promise."

Nicole looked into the car at Christopher.

"You're going to stay with him, right?"

"Yes."

Christopher brought me back home. All I could say on the way back was that I was sorry, over and over. He just drove without speaking.

"I'll be okay if you want to leave," I told him once he pulled into the driveway.

"No. I'm staying. Let's go inside."

We walked into the house.

"You want to watch television?" Christopher asked.

"Sure, if you do."

For the next few hours we laid in the bed watching different shows as it was getting dark outside.

"Really, it's okay if you want to go," I told him.

"No. I'm spending the night. Let's just go to bed."

We undressed in front of each other as we had time and time again over the past two years and got into bed. He laid down facing the wall with the dresser against it. I slid in as close as I could and put my arms around him. It was such a familiar feeling—having Christopher in my arms. I felt a sigh of relief inside. The feel of his skin against mine was like medicine at the moment. I just looked at the back of his head, full of dirty blond hair, at his neck and back as I held on tight to his stomach, my pelvis against his butt. I kissed the back of his neck, trying to stay awake as long as I could. The light had faded into darkness outside and I began to dread the sunrise that was inevitable. He would most likely leave in the morning and I did not want to see him walk out the door—afraid he would not return. Soon, I heard Christopher fall into sleep. His breathing was comforting and, within minutes, it engulfed me, too.

What must have been a few hours later, I woke up in a panic. I was relieved to see it was still dark outside. I got out of bed and went into the bathroom. I fell on my knees and vomited into the toilet with my hands grasping my stomach. I stayed in that position for a few moments, before getting up and cleaning myself up. Then, I brushed my teeth and gargled with mouthwash before quietly returning to bed. Christopher seemed to not have been disturbed by my exit from the bed. Then, he turned around and looked me in the eyes.

"Are you sick? I heard you throw up in the bathroom."

"No. I had a bad dream. More like a nightmare. You were with another guy."

He did not say a word. Christopher just kept looking at me. Then a few seconds later he pulled me in close to him, belly to belly and started kissing me on the lips passionately. I felt his erection against me. His arms were locked around me. Could this be happening, I thought? Suddenly I was filled with emotion, with so much love for him. He rolled on top of me. I felt the weight of his body against mine as he continued to kiss me, his tongue deep in my mouth.

"I want you," I whispered to him.

"Where's the lube?" he asked.

"In the drawer."

With the reach of my arm, I blindly searched for the handle with my fingers, managing to pull it halfway open. I fumbled around, feeling for the tube as Christopher was still kissing me. I was aroused, but still too upset to get fully hard. My heart was racing, filled with love for him.

"Put some on me," Christopher instructed.

He took the tube out of my hand instead, squirting out a large amount on his penis, and began stroking it.

"Sit on it," he instructed as he rolled over on his back.

I mounted him, feeling his penis slide inside me. There was a sharp pain.

"Easy. Give me a second," I asked.

I took a deep breath. The pain subsided as I lowered my body. Within seconds, he was fully inside. His thrusts were slow and cautious at first. Then he moved faster and faster up into me. Our roles were usually reversed, but it was the passion I wanted, the contact—to feel him and get as close to him as possible. It did not matter who was on the top or bottom at this point. I just wanted to be one with him. He put his hand behind my neck, pulling my face down to his, kissing my lips until they became red and swollen with passion. Then he flipped me over, still staying inside. Christopher moved his lips, kissing my neck until they reached my chest and began sucking on my nipples. I kissed the top of his head and felt his strong back with both my hands. The headboard repeatedly knocked against the wall as I felt every inch of him move in and out of me—his pelvis drives, strong and forceful. I did not want him to stop. I wanted to hold on to him as long as possible and feel every emotion the lovemaking afforded. Christopher's thrusts sped up and then slowed down, fast then slow, fast then slow, until they came like rapid fire. Days and nights could have passed. It was like being in a time warp. Then, suddenly without warning, he let out a cry. I felt his warm, thick semen shoot inside of me. He continued moving in and out after his ejaculation for another minute or so before stopping. I rested my body on top on his, looking at his face, into his eyes—those beautiful green eyes I had gazed into a millions times before. We both remained still, not speaking a word as I rested my hands on the light hair of his strong chest. I leaned down to kiss him again— those soft, beautiful lips against mine. I held the kiss as long as possible, longing for an eternity of night. After a few more moments, I grudgingly let him slide out as I rolled over to his side, praying the night would never end, and that daylight would never return to this part of the world.

Soon, he fell back asleep. I continued to stay awake looking at him and listening to his deep inhales and long exhales until they slowed, drifting Christopher into a quiet slumber. I resisted the persuasion of sleep itself, not wanting to miss out on a moment of being next to him. But I was soon overtaken by it, and the emotional exhaustion of the day.

I woke up about an hour later. The day's light was easing its way through the white shades of the windows. I saw it as an invasion. I felt sick. I rubbed my eyes and looked over at Christopher. He was naked, sitting against the headboard, his arms wrapped around his knees. I moved closer to him and reached out to touch his arm.

"Are you okay?" I asked.

"I don't know."

The sickness in my gut returned, this time bigger. I was afraid to ask anything else—afraid of the answers to the question I did not want to ask.

"What's wrong?" I mustered up the courage to ask.

"You scared me yesterday. I mean, I have never seen you in such a state. To want to kill yourself. What's wrong with you?"

"I was afraid of losing your love. Afraid of you walking out the door and taking it with you. Love is the only thing I have ever wanted in my life. Your love. Before you, there was nothing. Then the world opened up wide for me. I don't want to lose that. I don't want to lose you."

He was quiet for a few minutes.

"I'm overwhelmed with law school. I can't take this kind of pressure. I can't be responsible for your happiness or you wanting to kill yourself."

"It's not just about you. It's about my life before you. The life you saved."

I took a deep breath.

"You saw that scared little boy that has always been inside of me."

"That's just it. I can't save you."

"But you did. You're my Super Hero."

"Last night was a mistake," Christopher uttered.

"What do you mean?"

"Fucking you. I should not have fucked you."

"Don't say that. We made love last night like we have hundreds and hundreds of times before. Now you're telling me it was all a mistake?"

"I don't know what I'm saying."

"I love you. I would do anything for you. Haven't I shown you that over the past two years? The trips to Laguna Beach and to Miami. The day we drove over to San Diego so you could do that modeling shoot with the photographer when your parents told you to forget about modeling. Haven't I supported you in everything you wanted to do? What about the joint bank account I added to my portfolio so you would not have to worry about money? The twenty-five-hundred-dollar new laptop for law school?"

"You're throwing all that up to me. I don't want your money," Christopher said.

"I'm not throwing all those things up to you. I'm just reminding you that I have always been there for you. What is mine is yours. It's your money, too. You'll get most of it after I'm gone anyway."

"There you go talking about dying again. If you kill yourself it would destroy me. I'll have to kill myself, too," Christopher went on.

"I'm not talking about that in this instance, but more so of natural causes such as an accident," I clarified. "And what about my encouraging you to join the gay soccer team and going to all your games and everything else? The huge soccer party I gave you at the house? The beer pong table you asked me to make for it? Remember me calling you asking what color to paint it, and you said, red of course. What about all the baths we took together, talking in the hot water, looking into each other's eyes? What about all the times we held hands under the table at a restaurant and in the car? It's all gone now? I'll never get to hold you again, or kiss you or make love to my beloved? What about our dog, Dugan? You're just going to leave all that behind?" I questioned.

"I just don't want to talk about it," Christopher insisted.

"Okay. Just know I love you. You have made me happier than I have been in my whole life."

"I have a brief to finish for tomorrow. I need to get to the law library," Christopher told me.

"Okay, I understand."

And it was true. Everything I had was his, too. At least
I saw it that way. Several months after we had started dat-
ing, I was getting ready to fly back to Los Angeles. A few
nights before the trip I laid in bed wondering what would
happen if the plane crashed and I knew it was going to
happen. I wondered what would put my mind at peace, if
that was even possible, in that kind of situation, and I
never wanted to find out. My brother had enough money
and I did not want his children to profit from my demise.
In fact, I had already arranged that they would get nothing. My sister was getting the majority of the estate, but I
was afraid that she would just blow it and I did not want
any of my belongings to make it back to Warner Robins. I
was falling in love with Christopher and I wanted him to
get a good part of it. So, the next morning, I had my will
changed, leaving him over half of everything, a good part
to my sister and art to close friends, which was already in
the will. I sent a copy to Christopher in Athens and then
called him.

"You're going to get a copy of my will in the mail.
Don't freak out. I know we're still just getting to know
each other, but if something happens on my trip, I want
you to know how much you mean to me already."

He seemed surprised and just said, "Well, don't let
anything happen to you. I know I'll be in school all week
while you're away, but I miss you already."

My heart felt all warm and full. I was going out to in-
stall a commission for a client in the Hollywood Hills and
had arranged to be back by the weekend so I could be with
Christopher.

I watch Christopher dress, my heart grows bigger and

bigger like it is going to burst and explode all over the room. I put on my jeans and walk him out to the car like I had done a million times. We hug. He opens the door and gets in. I stand there until he rolls down the window and I lean in to kiss him again. I stand at the edge of the drive-way watching him drive away as he had done so many times, but he had always come back. The breath in my lungs is sucked out of me as I watch his car turn the cor-ner at the end of the street. I continue to stand there look-ing at the empty street, breathless; my heart seemed to stop beating. And I wondered if he was going to ever come back again—if he was ever coming back to me.

Well into the first week of January I started plan-ning—deciding that the plan of pulling the Jag into the studio would be the easiest way to go. I could sit in it with the top down and look at all the art I had finished and the pieces that would never be completed—like my life—stopped mid-way. The pills would make me fall asleep, and then the carbon monoxide would finish the job. If nothing else, it would be a poetic death for a sad soul and the tragic life of an artist comes to an end.

On January 12, 2009 I woke up in a panic. It was a Tuesday. I missed Christopher, unbelievably so. I felt like I had been on a drug, perhaps heroin, for two years and was suddenly cut off cold turkey by my drug dealer. I was going through withdrawal. I felt disposable, unwanted, a throwaway. Again, I missed everything about him. Every-thing! I could not stop thinking about how much I missed our long soaks in the bath. Our walks with Dugan to the coffee shop and the little monster jumping up on the table trying to drink our Mint Condition coffees. I missed

291

watching hours and hours of The O. C. television program on DVD in bed. I had gotten Christopher the entire gift set. I wanted to hold his hand under the table and in the car again. I wanted to make love to him again. I missed holding him in bed at night. My heart felt so fragile, so delicate, like an old piece of lace, once white, and made of the threads spun from the very cotton picked from the plants in the fields of my grandfather's farm by the old, unsteady hands of a distant relative; the lace now yellowed with tattered ends and loosened knots, having been hidden away in the bottom of an old dresser in years of darkness. Once exposed to the sunlight, it crumbled into dust—into the very dust from the ground from which it was grown.

I had been going to bed every night at 7 p.m. taking two or three sleeping pills to put me out, sometimes taking Benadryl, too, and praying God would trade my life with someone else's who wanted to live but was dying of cancer or AIDS, or someone who needed a heart transplant, but not sure my heart would do anyone any better than it was doing for me. That morning, I felt like the weight of the world was on my chest. I could not take in a full breath of air. I thought to myself, I can not live one more day—I can not face another morning. Not tomorrow or the day after or the day after that, or the next, much less next month, or next year.

Dugan was barking in his crate in the office, located in the front of the house. He is like an alarm clock. Seven-thirty every morning he is ready to get up if I do not let him sleep with me in the bed. The last few nights I had put him in his crate with his rubber toy stuffed with peanut butter. I haphazardly got dressed, putting on an old pair of jeans and a white T-shirt. As soon as I opened the crate, he ran for the back door. I led him to his enclosed area behind the studio that I had made to keep him from destroying the backyard and everything in it whether it were nailed down or not. I fixed his food.

I had the studio built four years ago, thinking that a two-car garage would up the resale value of my house, especially in Midtown, once I put it on the market when I was getting ready for my move to California before my mother first took ill. I had it built to match the house and decided to use it as my art studio until finally heading west. I had been painting in a room at the back of the house before. The studio had an opened pitched roof, four skylights, four tall side windows, a large picture window and a full-view door, as well as two rollup garage doors. The floor was concrete, and the studio was painted white top to bottom. It had a continuous eighteen-inch storage shelf on three sides that served as an easel on which to lean the art. I moved the large work table that was in the middle of the studio off to the side so the Jag would fit into the right side.

An hour later, I drove to the gas station a few blocks from the house to fill it up. The car radio was off. I had not listened to music since the break-up in fear of hearing all those sappy love songs, reminding me of what I had lost. Upon returning, I parked the Jag in the studio and lowered the top. I went back into the house and wrote Nicole a letter. I had met her in the spring of 2006. She was living in Athens then, commuting to Atlanta several days a week looking for a space to open an aerial dance studio. I told her to move in with me to save her time. She was only supposed to stay three months, just enough time to find her a place and for me to sell my house and move to California. Shortly after, that is when my mother got sick. Nicole ended up living with me for just over a year and we became great friends. In the letter, I wrote her I was sorry, and how much she meant to me, but it was time. In the letter I asked her to be there for Christopher and to fulfill my wishes with the house and the bank accounts. I reminded her I did not want a memorial service and to call Wil, a long-time friend and owner of the home Christopher and I had stayed in during our trip to the West Coast, to pick up my ashes the next time he was on his way to Laguna Beach. He knew where to spread them. I also included that I had boarded Dugan at the vet's and that Christopher could pick him up. I had already given Nicole my security codes to my bank accounts, and told her what I wanted to be done at the time she had agreed to be the executor of my will, so I paper-clipped the original will to the letter. I had given her a copy many months ago as I had Christopher. Then I wrote her a second letter that I was going to put out in the mail box. In it, I wrote her what I had done, or, rather, was about to do, and for her not to go to the house upon receipt. Rather, she was to call the police and inform them my body could be found in the studio. Then I wrote a note to Mace, a lifelong friend, to thank my friends, Alva and Wil, for loving me like a family. I was sorry and thanked him for all his love over the years. I wrote a short note to Christopher, expressing that he had nothing to do with my decision and that he should never blame himself—that I wished him the best in life. I wrote I was just sorry I could not have spent more time with him, but the pain and the loss were too gut-wrenching. I could not live another day without him, but that even if I had never met him the outcome would have most likely been the same. The last note was to my sister. In it, I wrote for her to keep going strong, to be the one that made it. I wrote I felt a sense of peace knowing that I would not have to face another tomorrow and falsely implying that the pills I had used were not the ones she had given me.

With all that done, I felt numb. I went back out to get Dugan and put him in his crate in my office; it was getting cold outside as the temperature was dropping. I coaxed him with his toy filled with peanut butter. Then I roamed around the house with no real purpose, stopping at the front door from time to time looking out to the street at the spot where Christopher would usually park his car. Then I went into my bedroom and looked at some framed pictures of Christopher on the dresser, before opening the top right drawer where I kept the sleeping pills and the prescriptions from the doctor. I started feeling anxious. I rattled through the different-sized bottles among my white underwear for the one with the Paroxetine. I took three and took a deep breath. Then I gathered up those containing the sleeping pills and popped two into my mouth. I opened several other drawers just to look at Christopher's T-shirts and soccer shorts. There was a neat stack of some of his underwear and a few pair of his socks. I walked over and opened the closet door. I ran my hands over several of his shirts that I had color coordinated, before pulling one off the hanger and holding it in my hands against my face. I breathed in deeply, smelling his scent still on it. Below on the floor was a pair of his shoes and one of his soccer balls. I rolled it out of the closet with my foot and kicked it, watching it as it made its way across the room and out into the hallway.

I placed his shirt on the bed, and laid down on top of it, remembering how I would not change the sheets after he left to drive back to college on Sunday nights or Mon-

day mornings until the following Friday, when he usually
returned to spend the weekends with me during his senior
year. I would meet him at the front door, pull our shirts up
to just below our chests as we kissed hello so our bellies
would touch. From the bed, I looked at the soccer ball just
outside the doorway of the bedroom. My eyes were wet
and swollen. I got up, taking his shirt with me, rubbing my
eyes with it on my way to the kitchen for a bottle of water
before going back to the studio. I dropped everything in
the passenger seat. I started looking at all the artwork—
remembering I had promised my Washington, D.C., art
rep at Urban Art Group that I would start on some pieces
for a landscape show in October. Then I thought about the
show I had there last year when Christopher and Dugan
went with me. We even took Dugan to the opening. He
was a bigger hit than the art. I moved a few pieces of art
around, pulling out the large piece I was doing of Christopher and leaned it on the shelf, unfinished—like our relationship. I had planned on doing a whole show of just images of him. This one was supposed to be the first in the
series. I stood in front of it, wishing things had ended up
differently. Then, I began wondering what his life was
going to be like—hoping it would be a great one. I wondered if anyone could possibly love him more than I did. I
figured he would hate me at first, but that hopefully, over
time, he would forgive me as my friends would.

An hour must have passed. Long murky, winter shadows stretched through the tall windows of the studio. I
knew the sun would be setting soon. I started to cry as I
closed the left garage door. I wiped my face with his shirt
again before opening the car door. I sat down in the
driver's seat, remembering that Christopher had driven me
to pick the Jag up somewhere in South Atlanta after I had

it shipped out during one of my stays in Los Angeles. I thought about how much fun I thought we were going to have driving around in it on nice sunny days. My heart felt like it was filling up with blood, getting bigger and bigger, with no way to release it. Again, all I knew was that I could not face another day. I turned the ignition on and rested my head back. I was not sure what I was doing, but had convinced myself I did not have any other choice. I was that scared little kid again not fully aware of the consequences, but feeling I was better off dead.

With the double exhaust system, the studio rapidly started filling up with fumes. I reached for the water bottle, still crying, wiping my eyes again with Christopher's shirt. I looked around the studio thinking about all the things I wanted to do with him—all the places I wanted us to travel to together. A few minutes must have passed, perhaps five, before I noticed one of Dugan's play toys on the shelf next to a painting. He had always hung out with me in the studio while I was painting, really more of a nuisance than a helper, trying to get into all my supplies. I would have to chase him around the work table and back yard to retrieve a screwdriver, hammer, or anything that he thought was a toy. Once I thought he was chewing on one of his bones, but at a second glance realized he had a large tube of black oil paint in his mouth. It was all over his face and neck and it took me hours to get him white again. Then I remembered all the times Christopher would come out the back door of the house and Dugan would run to him from the studio. They would play for a few minutes and then Christopher would come to hug and kiss me. I started to cough, my eyes began to sting, and I was already feeling sleepy. My mind started wandering more.

Strangely, my mother kept coming in and out of my

thoughts:

the early years;

the sweetness of her voice during simpler, happier times;

her full flowing skirts;

the smell of her Chanel No. 5;

the feel of her lips on my cheek;

her holding my hand helping me up the steps of the farmhouse.

Then the sad years: the sound of my father's hand slapping her around; his voice belting out orders; the sting of his belt on my legs as I kicked my feet at him; the tears running down my face; my father's blood on the rug and sofa, and on my hands; the bloody water in the bucket; my mother's screams of madness calling out for help in the middle of the night; her limp body sitting at the kitchen table with cigarette smoke encircling her; and her lying in the coffin.

I looked at the pill bottles and picked up one, then emptied its contents into my hand. I just looked at them, thirty or so green little capsules. I thought about the first time I kissed Christopher—how nervous I was—how soft his lips felt against mine. Then I heard my mother's voice calling me to come in for dinner. I noticed Dugan's toy again. I began coughing more, I thought about when Christopher and I drove to Oxford, Alabama, to get him when he was six weeks old. We had just gotten back from Laguna.

"Dugan," in a semi-foggy haze I thought, suddenly realizing I had forgotten to take him to the kennel. It will be at least two days before anyone finds him. The pills spilled out of my hand as I opened the car door, coughing my way through the thickening air to the door of the studio. "I have to get Dugan," I kept thinking as I made my way to the back door of the house.

He was sitting up in his crate, looking at me. He made a low bark. I sat on the floor of the office and started to cry again. My head was fuzzy, as I reached over to unlock the crate. Dugan ran out into my arms. I held on tightly to him as he squirmed, licking my face.

I smelled the scent of Chanel No. 5 in the air, and then I felt her behind me—my mother. The warm, tender feeling of her gentle hand rubbed over my back. The sensation ran through me. Then I heard her speak to me.

"I told you I would be back," she said. "You're not going to kill yourself."

Then I remembered the night I thought she had walked out of the Intensive Care Room, where she paused for a moment in front of me, looking into my eyes before she spoke the words, "Don't worry, I'll be back, Son." I looked down at the green braided ribbon on my left wrist, remembering the day I had put it on before putting one on her when she was in the coma. Then I realized that that hunter-green braided ribbon was my strand of hope—the hope I thought I had lost. She had come back to save me.

Epilogue

It was not the road my mother had planned to take, nor I, for that matter. We both have traveled a long way from the dust-covered dirt road from which it all started, and we have journeyed back to it. Our lives were similar in so many ways: our dreams, hopes and the personal pain that was seeded deep inside us from our ancestry. I came to understand the madness my mother had endured, especially while I searched out her personal story. She was, as I am, strong on the outside, but fragile beings under our skin. We never believed in ourselves enough, and never loved ourselves as others had. As mother and son, we had our struggles, mostly due to her drinking. It took me years to stop blaming my mother—for the drinking. In her drunken states, she would lash out, telling me she wished I had never been born. Today, I know she was lashing out at my father and mostly at the dreams she had lost on the way of her passage through life.

Yes, we are the same, my mother and I. I see her reflection in the mirror. The silhouette of her face, the shape of her eyes and lips are mine, as are her weaknesses and fears, strengths and courage. As I came to understand my mother, I realized I was powerless to free her from her past and its overbearing pain. Now I understand why her only solace was the bottle and the impermanent reprieve from the piercing, gut-wrenching ache—her life-long companion—that its contents afforded. At best, the burning liquor navigating its way down her throat toward her belly only diluted it.

As for me, I am not sure my mother will be able to save me a second time. That is in the future, and only it will tell where I will end up and how I will meet my end. The pages of that book have not been written. All I know at this juncture is that I have to leave my childhood behind. But first, before doing so, I have to soothe the fears of that sad little boy that was called Randy by his loving mother and put them to rest. One thing I am certain of is that I will never have to go back to the house where our lives were destroyed. And with that knowledge, I leave behind the ghost of my father that still wanders through the house on Shirley Drive, where I felt his presence every time I walked through the front door—even after thirty-four years and the last night I lay awake through a troubled night. He is trapped inside the walls which for years isolated us from the rest of the world—roaming in and out of the undersized, dingy rooms that concealed the childhood that was mine—a childhood which stunted my growth and left me feeling anything but human and kept a part of me child-like into my adult years.

A bad childhood is something you do not easily dismiss, or grow out of, like a pair of old jeans. If you have not lived it, then you will never know just how hard it is to walk away and never look back, especially when there are reminders all around you—like knick-knacks displayed on a mantel—and you yourself are the biggest reminder of them all. You are the biggest souvenir.

Everyone has a different way of getting over a dire experience, particularly if it has lasted a good part of a lifetime. A cancer would be easier to cure, or some growth that could be cut out of my body by a surgeon's scalpel. I thought my dire experience was over the day I walked into the living room and saw my father's blood. It is true something ended, but its conclusion did not end the pain; rather, something else began to breed inside of me that day that his blood covered my hands as I cleaned up a lasting reminder that would forever stain my soul.

He could have gone anywhere to do it: to a motel room, the woods, somewhere far away from where we lived. I can only imagine that, by not doing so, he wanted us to continue to suffer. So, he did it there. My father opened that door leading into a chilly, dark room when he took his own life—in the very place we had sat silently, as a family, watching the television—the only successful thing we managed to do as a family. Otherwise, the only thing that coupled us together was the blood that ran through his veins and out of the hole in the back of his head, the very blood on my hands that day.

I am not sure how I have survived this long without taking my own life just as my father had done. There have been times since then that I have been close. Death, my death, had been something I had thought about more than I should. I can not look over a high balcony without thinking about it; without thinking how easy it would be to climb over the railing and fall to my death. I hope that is all past me now, the thoughts of how I would do it and the array of scenarios, entertained at some of my lowest points when I would lay awake in my bed—the room filled with a soft light—as I thought of the most unproblematic and least messy way to do it—not wanting to leave mayhem as my father had done. It should be clean, with nothing for anyone to clean up. Easy.

But, dying is never easy. Or at least, this is what I have learned from what I have witnessed—from my father's blood and from watching life leave my precious mother's body. It took years for my father to die; years before he placed the barrel of the rifle between his lips and slid it deep into his throat. I still wonder if it was an act of courage or cowardice. At first, I thought it was his way of freeing us. But the very fact of where he did it made me believe it was the latter. As a child I had a sense he was not whole, there was something very deficient about him. There had always been an emptiness in his eyes—the very incompleteness I have felt in myself. My father had always been so outwardly strong and forceful, but in a cowardly way. He was an abuser of defenseless women and children. His last act of violence left my family scarred forever and opened that unspeakable door that leads to the act of playing God. On that lonely January day, I walked into that dark room, not wanting to return to the light of day—and I almost did not return.

My mother's spirit gave me hope again. It was the only thing that the farm or my father could not take from her. I am alive today because of that hope, and, no matter how microscopic it is within me, it is there resting on the tip of a sharp point of a needle that has pierced my heart. It is the same hope I saw on my mother's face as she stood at the window in the middle of winter looking for the first signs of the daffodils—looking for the first signs of hope.

So, like the daffodils combating the cold, and like those greyhounds chasing hope around and around and around, some other force must have kept it there inside of me. I know now that it was Mother who is responsible for keeping that hope in front of me. So, I will keep chasing it. Chasing it like the quicksilver, graceful dogs. Chasing it just like she had done as long as I am able.

By far, the experience of my mother's illness and passing is the hardest thing I have had to live through. I can not image anything worse or more heartbreaking. Since she first became ill, I have cried enough to fill a good-sized lake—in the car, driving back and forth between Warner Robins and Atlanta—during the long walks of solitude in the park—and for the countless hours curled up, like an orphaned baby, with a pillow in my arms, weeping, soaking it with tears of fear, sadness, pending loss, and so much regret.

Although I know there will be many more inescapable moments where I will break down and fall to my knees as I am reminded of the magnitude of her loss, I hope those tears will become ones of relief and peace knowing my mother is in a better place—finally in the comfort of God, where a lifetime of pain and sorrow is no longer, having been soothed away by a single kiss from his loving lips. She had a life—a birth and a death. She took air into her lungs for seventy-five years; and, in her last hours, she gasped for every degree of it. She was a baby, a girl, a teenager, a daughter, a sister, a cousin, a young woman, a wife, a lover, a mother, a widow, a lover again, an old woman, a grandmother, and a great-grandmother. Her life was a roller-coaster of emotions. From an early age she met heartache and desperation. She felt confined in a small world and longed to cross the boundaries that her birth set for her and which she believed had imprisoned her. But she believed in me and I truly trust that her spirit returned to keep me from meeting the same end as her husband, my father.

The second hardest thing I have experienced in my life is the loss of Christopher's love. My sweet Christopher, I can only hope that one day you will see again what you once saw in me. It took me fifty years to find love. I can honestly say I have loved no other more than I do you. The tremendous love I felt from you equals the heartache you have left me with. Love is forever; at least mine is. Christopher—you are my California.

I am sure I will venture back to Rushing Road from time to time and walk it with her beside me.

I will remember the hopes and dreams that were seeded among the white fields of cotton, and remember the life she gave up for me. From this day forward I will spend my time fulfilling my own dreams in honor of the ones she had lost.

And by doing so, I know I am fulfilling one of her dreams—my happiness.

"I'm okay, if you're okay."

Rest in eternal peace, my dear mother.

I know everything good I do comes from you and from your struggles in the white fields of cotton—Alabama Snow.

Acknowledgments

A very special thanks to
Patricia
Kelly
Bob
Mary
Mace
Cory
Nicole
Harvey
Michael
Monte
Neil
Susan Z.
Dawn
Cheryl
Richard
Scott
Wil
Rusty
Alva
Lee
Pat
Rose

I could not have gotten through this journey of writing this story without your love and support. You all played a part in saving my life.

CPSIA information can be obtained at www.ICGtesting.com
Printed in the USA
LVOW07s1110080116

469827LV00024B/176/P